W9-BOF-085

PORTFOLIO / PENGUIN

SHARK TALES

Barbara Corcoran's credentials include straight Ds in high school and college, and twenty-two jobs by the time she turned twenty-three. It was her next job, founding The Corcoran Group real estate company, that would make her one of the most successful entrepreneurs in the country. She is the real estate contributor for NBC's *Today* show and is a Shark on ABC's *Shark Tank*. She lives in New York City with her husband and two children. Visit her at barbaracorcoran.com.

Bruce Littlefield is a best-selling author and lifestyle expert. His brand of American fun is seen on the *Today* show, *The Early Show*, and *The View*. Visit him at brucelittlefield.com.

Praise for Barbara Corcoran and *Shark Tales*

"[*Shark Tales*] will leave you laughing and crying, but most of all confident that you too can make this world of business work for you."
—Gail Evans, author of *Play Like a Man, Win Like a Woman*

"Corcoran is a lightning bolt of energy caught in a five-foot-six frame."
—*USA Today*

"Barbara Corcoran may be New York's real estate diva, but it's her home-maker mother to whom she looks for inspiration."
—*Crain's New York Business*

"A witty memoir and a powerful guidebook on how to get ahead. . . . An emotionally charged and intellectually energetic book, which will give people ideas on how to motivate, invigorate and otherwise encourage any group that they lead, and organization they build." —Bookreporter.com

"Entrepreneurs' visions don't always translate well to the page, but Corcoran's book . . . is cleanly written and humorous. The squeaky-clean Waltons-esque descriptions of Corcoran's family lend it an almost folksy feel."
—*Fortune Small Business*

Shark Tales

How I Turned $1,000 into

a Billion Dollar Business

Barbara Corcoran

with Bruce Littlefield

Also known as *Use What You've Got* and *If You Don't Have Big Breasts, Put Ribbons on Your Pigtails*

PORTFOLIO / PENGUIN

PORTFOLIO/PENGUIN

Published by the Penguin Group
Penguin Group (USA) Inc., 375 Hudson Street, New York, New York 10014, U.S.A.
Penguin Group (Canada), 90 Eglinton Avenue East, Suite 700, Toronto, Ontario,
Canada M4P 2Y3 (a division of Pearson Penguin Canada Inc.)
Penguin Books Ltd, 80 Strand, London WC2R 0RL, England
Penguin Ireland, 25 St Stephen's Green, Dublin 2, Ireland
(a division of Penguin Books Ltd)
Penguin Group (Australia), 250 Camberwell Road, Camberwell, Victoria 3124, Australia
(a division of Pearson Australia Group Pty Ltd)
Penguin Books India Pvt Ltd, 11 Community Centre, Panchsheel Park,
New Delhi – 110 017, India
Penguin Group (NZ), 67 Apollo Drive, Rosedale, North Shore 0632, New Zealand
(a division of Pearson New Zealand Ltd)
Penguin Books (South Africa) (Pty) Ltd, 24 Sturdee Avenue, Rosebank,
Johannesburg 2196, South Africa

Penguin Books Ltd, Registered Offices:
80 Strand, London WC2R 0RL, England

First published in the United States of America as *Use What You've Got* by Portfolio,
a member of Penguin Putnam Inc. 2003
Paperback edition with the title *If You Don't Have Big Breasts, Put Ribbons on Your
Pigtails* published 2004
This revised edition published 2011

5   7   9   10   8   6   4

Copyright © Barbara Corcoran and Bruce Littlefield, 2003, 2011
All rights reserved

Illustrations by John Segal

LIBRARY OF CONGRESS CATALOGING IN PUBLICATION DATA
Corcoran, Barbara (Barbara Ann).
Shark tales : how I turned $1,000 into a billion dollar business / Barbara Corcoran ;
with Bruce Littlefield.
p.   cm.
Rev. ed. of: Use what you've got : and other business lessons I learned from my mom /
Barbara Corcoran with Bruce Littlefield. 2003
Includes index.
ISBN 978-1-59184-418-1
1. Corcoran, Barbara (Barbara Ann).   2. Women real estate agents—United States—
Biography.   3. Real estate business—United States.   I. Littlefield, Bruce (Bruce
Duanne)   II. Corcoran, Barbara (Barbara Ann) Use what you've got.   III. Title.
HD278.C67A3   2011
333.33092—dc22
[B]   2010045012

Printed in the United States of America
Set in Avenir

For Mom, who taught me to believe in myself,
and for Dad, who taught me how to have fun.

Contents

Contents

Introduction

The story of my billion-dollar business starts like this: I borrowed $1,000 from a friend. Okay, I didn't borrow it. He gave it to me. And he wasn't a friend. He was a boyfriend. But when I moved into my first New York City apartment, on East 86th Street, with two roommates, I did have $1,000 to start a real estate company.

It seemed so simple. There'd be virtually no overhead! I'd probably rent two, maybe even three apartments a day, and we'd be running at a profit by the second Sunday of every month. "All the rest will be gravy," I told my new business partner and boyfriend, Ramòne Simòne.

"And we'll share that gravy evenly," he added. Or *almost* evenly—51 percent for him and 49 percent for me. After all, he explained, he was the one risking the money.

The CORCORAN Family

JOSEPHINE
NANA

FLORENCE
MOM

EDWIN JR.
DAD

DENISE
DENISE
The BEAST

BARBARA
BOOGIE BOOGIE
BARBARA

EDWIN III
EDDIE
SPAGHETTI

ELLEN
ELLEN
WATERMELON

JOHN
JUMP JOHNNY
JUMP

THOMAS
TIPPY
TOE TOMMY

MARY JEAN
MARY JEAN
The BEAN

MARTIN
MARTY
JOE

JEANINE
JEANINE
The QUEEN

FLORENCE
FRED

BUDDY

PRINCE I

PRINCE II

ZHA-ZHA

SAM

PART ONE

10 Kids, 1 Bath

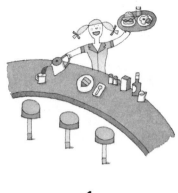

1

If You Don't Have Big Breasts,
Put Ribbons on Your Pigtails

My mother always says my memory is bigger than my life. Well, here's what I remember.

I grew up beneath a giant cliff on the bottom floor of a three-story house in New Jersey. It was a sliver of a town called Edgewater, and it was two blocks wide and one mile long, just across the Hudson River from Manhattan. My house was easy to find—it was the brown clapboard sitting right below the gigantic *L* of the flickering Palisades Amusement Park sign—and through most of my childhood it was home to twenty-one people.

Uncle Herbie and Aunt Ethel lived on the top floor with their two teen daughters. Nana Henwood lived in the front half of the second floor; the Roanes and their two Peeping Tom sons lived in the back. My family, the Corcorans, lived on the ground floor—the best floor, we thought. We were six girls sharing the middle room, which we called "the girls' room," and four boys sharing the back room, called "the boys' room." My parents, Florence and Ed, slept on the black vinyl Castro convertible in the living room.

But I never really saw my mother sleep. In fact, she sat down only during dinner and later for about three minutes in the tub of our one bathroom. Although Mom was perennially pregnant, she was always on the move—a blurry blue Sears housedress topped by a wavy blond perm and supported by two sturdy speed-walking legs. She had bulging purple varicose veins that grew with each child, and I was always worried that they were going to pop. But they didn't.

On any given day, Mom could be found in one of two places: the outside landing, where she hung the laundry, or the kitchen, where she jogged between the ironing board and the oven. It seemed my mother could do a hundred things at once, all the while keeping at least one of her blue eyes on her ten children.

"Watch yourself, Eddie!" she'd shout down from the landing to my oldest brother in the side yard. "Remember, you're a born leader and all the boys are watching you!" Then she'd vroom down the fourteen wooden steps, hip the laundry basket through the banging screen door into the kitchen, and dump everything onto the table.

"You're the absolute *best* helper, Ellen," she'd say as my eager sister did the folding. "You're going to make a *wonderful* mother!"

Shortly after noon, Mom would begin preparations for dinner, served nightly at six o'clock sharp. "Barbara Ann!" she'd yell down the basement stairs as she peeled potatoes. "Come on up here and take Florence, Tommy, and Mary Jean. They need some entertainment and if you're going to be a star, you'll need to practice."

And that was my mother's genius. She kept her house going by putting her finger on the special gift she saw in each of her children and making each and every one of us believe that that gift was uniquely ours. Whether it was true or not, we all believed it.

I was wiping my counter at the Fort Lee Diner the first time Ramòne Simòne walked in. It was a slow night, with very few customers, and the other waitress, Gloria, had them all. Gloria was a dead ringer for Dolly Parton. She had a bleached-blond swirl of cotton candy hair and two breasts that were the specialty of the house. She and the dynamic duo had the power to lure men off the street, even when they weren't hungry. Watching the twins bounce around the restaurant had become the local sport in Fort Lee. Gloria could hip her way through the kitchen doors carrying two cups of coffee stacked on top of each breast and two more in each hand, never spilling a drop.

I was watching Gloria work her front section one night and, in an effort to feel busy, was washing the Formica in front of me with a soggy white rag. The double aluminum doors at the far end of the diner opened and in walked my destiny. With his olive skin, jet black hair, and blue aviator shades, he looked nothing like the working-class customers who frequented the place. He was different, probably from a land very far away. I figured at least across the river.

I had seen his crisp, white collar and rich dark suit on only one other person in my twenty-one years—Irvin Rosenthal, the elderly owner of Palisades Amusement Park. The famous park hovered atop the cliff above our house like a blinking, whirring spaceship. When we were kids, Mr. Rosenthal drove through Edgewater in his black limousine handing out free ride tickets to all the children in town. We ran up to his car like chickens to the feet of a farmer's wife, each of us hoping to get more than our fair share of tickets. In his dark suit and crisp white shirt, Mr. Rosenthal was like a king, and we all knew he was rich. Besides the fact that he owned the amusement park, he just smelled different.

Ramòne smelled different, too. I could tell even from across the room and over the thick aroma of frying bacon and eggs. Instead of asking to sit in Gloria's station, he looked at my boss at the door and, with a quick lift of his chin, nodded toward me, the young innocent behind the counter. He walked across the diner, strutting like a pigeon, and my eyes met his blue aviator shades. *Finally*, I thought, as he took a seat at the second stool, *an interesting customer.*

He ordered a cup of tea, and as I zipped in and out of the swinging kitchen door, he sipped it, watching me work my counter.

I loved my counter. It was my territory, and everything there was under my control. There were nine stools and every third one had a setup complete with glass sugar container, ketchup bottle, salt and pepper shakers, and a tin dispenser of white napkins. Stuck behind the counter face-to-face with customers, I often was their dinner companion, and I loved every minute of it, especially entertaining them with conversation.

Ramòne told me he was from the Basque Country. I didn't know if Basque was a town in New Jersey or not, and I suppose my face gave me away. It wasn't just *any* place in Spain, he explained; it was the upper echelon of French-Spanish society. He said his father had blond hair and blue eyes, just like mine, and he said he liked the red ribbons on my pigtails. I smiled, spritzing the top of the napkin tins with Windex and shining them extra well with a paper towel.

The man from the Basque Country left sixty-five cents on the counter and offered me a ride home. I didn't need to weigh the options: Walk the five blocks to the number 8 Lemoine Avenue bus or be driven home by him. "I'm finished at ten," I blurted.

Ramòne was parked outside in a yellow Lincoln Continental, the kind with the hump on the back. I took the diner's concrete steps two at a time and climbed into a car very different from any I'd ever seen. The soft seats felt like talcum powder against my legs—nothing like the crunchy seats of Dad's blue station wagon.

We headed ten minutes down the hill and pulled up to the curb in front of my house. Ray—he said I could call him Ray—followed me up the concrete steps, through the front door, and into our living room. I suggested he sit on the black vinyl sofa where my parents slept at night. Within seconds, he was surrounded by a blur of ten blond-haired, blue-eyed, cookie-cutter kids. I introduced Ramòne Simòne from the Basque Country to my parents and they hated him on sight, especially my mom, who, contrary to her normally welcoming ways, wanted the Dark Knight out of her house as quickly as possible. "He's much older than you, Barbara" is all I remember her saying after he left.

Ray waited outside the diner every night and gave me a ride home. I guess you could say we were dating, though I didn't think of the rides that way. He told me he was a big real estate developer and built houses in every town in New Jersey except mine. I learned that he was ten years older than I was and divorced with three daughters. To me, it all added to the intrigue.

A few months later, Ray said a smart girl like me should be living in the Big City, and to get me started, he offered to pay for a week at the Barbizon Hotel for Women, on Manhattan's Upper East Side. To my mother's shock and dismay, I jumped at his offer and packed my black ribbed sweater, two pleated skirts, navy blue peacoat, and my new pair of Christmas pajamas. When I carried my suitcase down, Mom was standing next to the living room radiator sorting socks.

"Now, Barbara," she said, pushing my bangs away from my eyes and looking out the front door toward the street, "don't you be fooled by that fancy car! It's meaningless. You're a nice girl and you know right from wrong. And remember, if you change your mind, you should head right home."

"I know, I know, Mom," I said, giving her a quick peck on the cheek and a one-armed hug. I hurried down the steps and climbed into Ray's yellow Lincoln with the nice leather seats. I felt the same mixture of fear and excitement I did every time the Cyclone clicked toward the top of the big hill. I didn't say a word as Ray revved the car's engine and turned up the hill, but I took one last look back at the house sitting beneath the *L* of the Palisades Amusement Park sign.

Ray gave me $100 to go buy myself a "real New York outfit." I bought a purple one—a stretchy lavender lace top, lavender corduroy bell-bottoms with six lavender buttons on the hip, and a pair of lace-up, knee-high lavender suede boots. I walked out of Bloomingdale's completely purple and proudly paraded up Lexington Avenue singing, *"Hey there! Georgy Girl, swinging down the street so fancy free . . ."* I knew I was lookin' good and needed only two more things to stay in New York City: a job and an apartment.

The next morning, I put on my new outfit and applied for a receptionist position with the Giffuni Brothers company, on East 83rd Street. The Giffuni Brothers were wealthy New York landlords who owned a dozen apartment buildings in Manhattan and Brooklyn. The woman interviewing me explained I'd be in charge of greeting every tenant who phoned with a perky "Good morning, Giffuni Brothers." It seemed easy enough, and by the end of the day, I had landed the receptionist job; by the end of the week I had found an apartment three blocks away and two girls to share the rent. I moved my suitcase out of the Barbizon Hotel.

My Giffuni Brothers stint introduced me to Manhattan real

estate. I wore my purple outfit eight days a week and probably said, "Good morning, Giffuni Brothers" eight hundred times a day. But after a few months of "Good morning, Giffuni Brothers," I eagerly gave Ray my "no overhead" spiel about running at a profit by the second Sunday of every month. Ray gave me the $1,000 to start a real estate company, and I quit my receptionist job. We decided to name the new company Corcoran-Simone. Ray said his investment entitled him to 51 percent of the interest, and my job was to run the office day-to-day so he could continue to build houses in New Jersey.

My old boss, Joseph Giffuni, offered to let me rent out one of his apartments and said he'd pay me a whole month's rent as a commission if I could find him a good tenant. He showed me the list of eleven apartments he had for rent, and I picked 3K, the cheapest one-bedroom on the list.

I created my makeshift Corcoran-Simone office on the sofa my roommate had borrowed from her parents. My newly installed pink Princess phone sat silent on the double-tiered mahogany end table, and I stared bleary-eyed at the Sunday *New York Times* classified ads. According to my count, there were exactly 1,246 one-bedroom apartments advertised. The ads were five or six lines long and the apartments were all priced between $320 and $380 a month for rent. I noticed the best ads among the lot were the splashy ones with the bigger, bolder headlines like FABULOUS 3! RIV VU 1 BR. TRIPLE MINT!!! followed by a long list of superlatives.

I worked out the numbers on my steno pad and realized that the big ads were bigger than my budget, so I decided to keep my ad to four lines or fewer each week in order to make Ray's $1,000 last a whole month. *But how*, I wondered, *can I make my little ad stand out among the biggies and how am I going to catch someone's eye?* I figured I needed a gimmick.

Stretching my neck and looking up from the paper, I thought about my job at the Fort Lee Diner. *Ah, Gloria! Now, she had a gimmick.* On my first day at the diner, I could see Gloria had assets I'd never have, and I went home to fret to my mother: "And when we weren't busy, Mom, my counter was plain empty. Even when Gloria's station was completely filled, men were *still* waiting to sit with Gloria and not me."

"Barbara Ann, stop your whining!" Mom said, as she simultaneously balanced baby Florence on her hip and hung a sheet on the line. "You're going to have to learn to use what you've got, and you've got a great personality. Since you don't have big breasts, why don't you tie some ribbons on your pigtails and just be as sweet as you are?"

And that's how Ray found me two years later, wearing red ribbons on my pigtails and offering a cheerful alternative to the big-breasted, tiny-waisted Fort Lee sensation. I considered it a personal victory when a customer walked into the diner and asked to sit with "Pigtails." I learned that men are just as attracted to the innocent virgin as they are to the blond bombshell. A simple gimmick pulled them to my counter, and my sweet-talking kept them coming back.

Sitting alone in my apartment with the *New York Times* spread open on my lap, I thought about Mom's advice for competing with Gloria, and I knew I needed an attention grabber for apartment 3K. *How*, I asked myself, *can I put ribbons on a typical one-bedroom in four lines or less and make it stand out from the other 1,246 apartments?*

I took a deep breath and picked up my pink Princess phone. "Hello, Mr. Giffuni," I began. "I've been thinking about your one-bedroom on the third floor, and I think I have a way to rent it for twenty dollars more each month." I had his attention. I told him how apartment 3K's living room was like every other living room in every other apartment in every other building in New York and convinced him that if he put up a wall separating the living room from the dining alcove, he'd really have something different! Mr. Giffuni hesitated and then said he'd have the wall installed that week. I phoned my ad into the paper.

The following Sunday, my first four-line ad (**bold** print counted for two lines) appeared in the *New York Times*:

1 BR + DEN $340

Barbara Corcoran,

212-355-3550

It wasn't a big ad like the others, but it offered something more. Why would *anyone* settle for a one-bedroom when for a similar price they could get a one-bedroom with a den?

That Sunday, the calls started rolling in. And on Monday I rented my first apartment.

2

Paint the Rocks White and the Whole Yard Will Look Lovely

October 1973. New York City.

I held my first commission check in my hand. *Three hundred and forty dollars!* I was standing on the corner of 83rd and First with the check and Mr. Giffuni's list of eleven new apartments for rent. It was October 17, New York was already turning cold, and the navy blue peacoat I had brought from New Jersey looked just like a navy blue peacoat I had brought from New Jersey. "I'm going to take this money and buy myself the best coat in New York," I told myself triumphantly.

I held up the check again as if it couldn't be real and looked at the number: $340.00! I'd seen only one check that was bigger in my entire life, and that was during my dad's one short stint running his own business.

1959. Edgewater, New Jersey.

One Monday night, Dad came to the dinner table and announced, "I'm happy to tell you kids that today I quit my job, and I'm starting my *own* business!" He looked really excited. "I won't be working for stupid Mr. Stein as his press foreman anymore!" he bragged. "And I'm naming my new company—listen to this—Pre-Press Preparations."

We all listened as Dad laid out his business plan, ten wide-eyed kids and one very worried, wide-eyed mother.

"From now on I'll be known as Edwin W. Corcoran, the *president* of Pre-Press Preparations," Dad continued. "And I'll also be the company's one-man sales force, but I'll use a pseudo name for phoning my customers." My sister Ellen asked what a "sudo-name" was, and Dad demonstrated with a would-be sales call: "Hello there. This is Paul Peterson of Pre-Press Preparations calling for Edwin Corcoran the president. . . ." I could see red blotches forming in the *V* of Mom's blue housedress, a well-known warning signal around our house.

Dad explained how his new company would design and also make all kinds of cardboard boxes. He picked up the Mueller Dairies milk carton from the table and said, "For instance, if

Mr. Mueller hired me, I would decide how big his carton should be, I'd pick the colors, and I'd even draw the cows! I'd also find the right factory to make his cartons. Yep, at Pre-Press Preparations we do it all!"

Within the week, Paul Peterson had sold his first client on a job to design a belt buckle box, and President Edwin W. Corcoran asked my brother Tommy and me to sit at his new drafting table and draw buckles with his new black Enco drafting pen. We drew six different designs; Dad cut them out, rubber-cemented them onto his white cardboard prototype, and sent them to press.

The following week, Dad came to the dinner table and we bowed our heads as he recited our usual prayer much faster than usual: "Bless us, Our Lord, for these our gifts which we are about to receive from-thy-bounty-through-Christ-Our-Lord. Amen!"

"Amen!" we agreed, and raised our heads to find Dad holding up a small blue paper in both hands, the same way Father Galloway held his golden chalice on Sundays. With great fanfare, he passed the blue paper around the table so everyone could have a look.

We each stared in awe at what appeared to be a check with a lot of zeros following the number one. It was Marty Joe who figured it out first.

"Why, it's a *thousand dollars*!" he said.

"Yup! That's right, kids!" Dad shouted. "We're RICH! And we're GOING ON VACATION!"

The next morning, my mother packed ten kids, ten bathing suits, and ten tuna fish on Wonder Bread into our blue station wagon, and we headed to Asbury Park. We had never stayed in a real hotel, and our one-week vacation at the Brighton Beach Hotel proved to be the most exciting week of our entire childhood.

One month later, Paul Peterson had been let go, Edwin W. Corcoran was out of business, and we were eating on credit from Bubsy's Grocery Store.

I looked back down at my first commission check and pondered, *Should I take the money and splurge on a new coat, or shouldn't I?* Remembering that my dad's first check as his own boss had been his last and that it had taken him ten months to find a new job as a press foreman, I decided I'd better not. Stuffing the check and the apartment list in my bag, I headed back to my apartment.

The building's super was perched at his usual post next to the mailboxes. "Good morning, Mr. O'Rourke," I chirped as I breezed past the potbellied, red-faced Irishman. He reminded me of Maggie O'Shay, from Edgewater. Mr. O'Rourke rightfully boasted of running "the cleanest building in all New York," just as Mrs. O'Shay claimed to keep "the cleanest house in Edgewater."

1957. Edgewater.

Although there wasn't a garden club in Edgewater, Mrs. O'Shay acted as its self-appointed president. She paced up and down Undercliff Avenue inspecting each yard while doling out her neighbors' secrets as though they were hers to give.

Mrs. O'Shay watched with raised eyebrows as my mother tried time and time again to spruce up our yard, and time and time again met only with failure. One spring, Mom laboriously stacked the yard's rocks to form a retaining wall, only to find it slowly eroding as we took the larger rocks to use as roast beefs in our pretend grocery store.

Next, Mom planted grass, only to learn grass doesn't grow very well on a rock-strewn hill shaded by a giant oak tree. Then, she dug thirty-six holes to plant a gladiolus garden. She dusted the bulbs with bonemeal and placed each one carefully in its nest. The next morning, the gladiolus bulbs were sitting beside their holes as though they had never been planted. After Mom's roll call yielded nothing but frustrating *not-me*'s, Prince, our collie-wolf-Chihuahua mix, was found guilty of digging for bones.

With stubborn determination, my mother dug thirty-six new holes and spent all of June watering, weeding, and waiting. Finally, one hot day in July, the green stalks began to unfurl their hot-pink and bright orange petals. It happened to be the same day Mom came home from the hospital with her ninth baby, Jeanine. Timmy Tom, the skinny five-year-old Harrison kid, greeted her at our kitchen screen door with a huge bouquet of her nearly opened gladiolus. "These are for you and your new baby, Mrs. Corcoran!" he said as he handed my mother the three months of hard work he had plucked from her yard.

Timmy Tom's flower delivery sent my mother right over the edge and down to the Edgewater hardware store. She came home with a gallon of Sherwin-Williams paint and an idea. She grabbed her yellow Fuller scrub brush and a bucket of water and called all of us into the side yard. We spent the afternoon scrubbing the roast-beef-size rocks while Mom followed behind us with her can of semigloss white. That night, we pressed our faces to the side yard window to admire the rocks that glistened brighter than the backyard fireflies.

Early the next morning, Mrs. O'Shay screeched to a halt in front of our house. "Oh! What a lovely yard you have, Mrs. Corcoran!" she cooed, admiring the ordinary rocks turned extraordinary. "What a truly lovely yard!" My mother smiled and waved proudly from the front steps, and that was the moment a new family tradition was born. Every spring thereafter, Mom gathered her children, a can of semigloss white, and her scrub brush, and we would all spend the day washing and swabbing a fresh coat of paint on the rocks in our truly lovely yard.

As I stepped into my apartment I felt the Giffuni Brothers' check burning a hole in my pocket. *Should I buy a new coat or shouldn't I?* I looked down at my lavender Georgy Girl outfit; I knew it had walked down the street too many times to still look fancy-free. *Should I or shouldn't I?* Well, I decided, if Mom could cover her old rocks with a coat of white paint, I could certainly cover *my* old outfit with a new coat!

I hightailed it down to First National City Bank to cash my check and made a beeline for Fifth Avenue. I was going to buy myself the *best* coat in the *best* store on the *best* block in all New York!

I asked the red-suited doorman at Bergdorf Goodman where I could find ladies' coats and took the gold-paneled elevator to the second floor. The elevator opened, and I tripped into a full city block of new coats. A well-clad saleswoman offered her help, but I was too intimidated to accept her offer and thought of a really original response: "No, thanks, I'm just looking." I puffed up my chest and dove straight into the sea of a thousand coats.

Suddenly, I spotted her from across the room. She was the flashiest one in the whole place. There was nothing plain about her. She had curly brown and white fur around a high mandarin collar and a pair of matching cuffs. Her wool was thick, laid in an oversize brown and white herringbone pattern. Down her front she had at least a dozen diamond-shaped buttons chiseled out of what looked like real bone. Each button hooked through its own loop. Her huge shoulder pads rode high and her hem swung low, almost touching the polished wood floor. Everything about her screamed, "HERE I AM!" And for $319 plus tax, she was mine.

My new coat became my signature piece and I never took it off. In it, I not only looked successful, I *felt* successful. My curious customers asked what kind of fur it was, and since I'd never spoken to the saleslady, I had no idea. "It looks a lot like my old dog, Prince," I'd joke. For the next two years, I marched in and out of buildings up and down Manhattan wearing my expensive coat and flaunting my new image for all it was worth.

3

If the Sofa Is Ripped,
Cover It with Laughter

One month later, on a cold November day, I arrived home to find a white envelope stuffed under our apartment door.

I opened it and read:

N.Y.C. DEPARTMENT OF HOUSING
NOTICE

11-12-73

FOR: Barbara Corcoran, **Tenant**

FROM: Campagna Holding Corp., **Landlord**

RE: **Premises known as** 345 East 86th Street

Apartment 9F

City of New York, New York 10028

NOTICE IS HEREB`Y GIVEN under the provisions of Chapter 186, section 12 of New York Laws, and those claiming under you to deliver up and quit the premises you presently hold as the tenant of Campagna Real Estate (known as landlord) no later than 11-30-1973. **Failing such vacating, legal action shall be commenced to evict you.**

"*. . . legal action shall be commenced to evict you?*" I reread aloud. "Evict *me*?" I staggered into the elevator, clutching the notice in my hand. I went downstairs and found Mr. O'Rourke next to the mailboxes. "Mr. O'Rourke," I sputtered, "I just found this eviction notice under my door and it doesn't make any sense! I know my rent is paid! I always collect it from Jackie and Sandi and send the checks in myself *before* the first of the month. I'm *never* late. This is some kind of mistake!" I waited for his response, clutching the notice even tighter.

"You'll best be talkin' to the landlord" was all Mr. O'Rourke said as he walked away, leaving me standing alone in the lobby.

At nine thirty the next morning I walked into the white brick office building at 770 Lexington Avenue. A dusty secretary reluctantly showed me into John Campagna's office. It was decorated in a mix of red velvet and the darkest, shiniest wood I had ever seen. My landlord was sitting at his desk. He was young and shockingly handsome. I watched him take note of my impressive coat. He offered to take the coat, but I was nervous and felt stronger in it, so I said that I was cold and I'd prefer to keep it on, thank you. He offered me a seat.

I sank into the red leather chair and started immediately: "I'm sure there must be some mistake, Mr. Campagna, because I received this eviction notice and I *know* my rent is paid. You see, I always collect the rent from my two roommates by the twenty-fifth of every month and enclose their two checks with mine in the rent envelope and mail it never a day later than the twenty-sixth of the month. It must arrive at your office by either the twenty-seventh or twenty-eighth, I'm sure never later than the twenty-ninth." He sat tapping a pen on his black leather desk pad, returning absolutely no expression, so I kept talking. "Mr. Campagna, we never play loud music, and never, ever leave food around. We've never had roaches—not even one."

Mr. Campagna shifted slightly in his chair but still said nothing. I felt I was wrestling with air.

I talked faster. "I've never, ever done anything wrong in my life and would consider myself a fine tenant in every way. I'm proud to be a fine tenant in your very fine building, Mr. Campagna."

Still no reaction.

"Mr. O'Rourke tells me you and your very fine wife and your two fine sons also live in your very fine building." As I stumbled through these last fine words, I realized my mandarin fur collar had overtaken my nose and was interfering with my speech. I took a quick look left, then right, and saw that my shoulder pads had been inching up and were now level with my ears. Mr. Campagna sat quietly, staring at a fast-talking blond tuft of hair and two desperate blue eyes.

Finally, he leaned back in his big leather chair and spoke slowly. "You have had a lot of traffic coming in and out of your apartment, Miss Corcoran, both during the day and evening hours." I agreed that I did have a lot of customers and said that my business relied totally on word of mouth. I added that I was new at it and hoped to have a lot more customers in the future. He looked shocked, almost to the point of horror.

"You're dressed rather *sophisticated* for such a young girl," he said, examining the bone buttons of my coat and fidgeting with his pen.

And that's when it hit me.

"Mr. Campagna!" I exclaimed, my mouth wide open in disbelief. "You. Think. I'm. A *prostitute*?!"

He said nothing.

"Oh, Mr. Campagna, if you knew my mother and knew how I was raised," I told him. "Why, Mr. Campagna, I'm almost a nun!"

Dinnertime. Edgewater.

Dinner at our house was an event—an event we were required to attend. At six o'clock sharp, we gathered around the plywood-covered table that grew larger with every new child, and took our usual seats. I sat at the foot of the table, near the bathroom, though I liked to think of it as the head of the table. Mom was to my left and between us was Jeanine's high chair.

Tonight, like every other night, Mom went around the table asking each child, "And how was your day today?" Mom always circled the table clockwise, starting with Ellen and ending with me.

"And how was *your* day today?" Mom asked Denise, who was sulking over her dinner. "You look worried. What's wrong?"

"Nothing," she answered adamantly.

"Nothing" was not an acceptable answer at my mother's table. We all stared at Denise, knowing Mom wasn't moving on until Denise changed her answer. "My new boyfriend is coming to the house later tonight!" Denise blurted out.

"Why, that's lovely," Mom responded. "Will he be coming soon? We certainly have enough spaghetti for him. What's the boy's name?"

"Bruce," Denise declared. "And he's rich. And he's going to see that we're not!"

We all slurped our spaghetti more slowly.

"He's going to come and see our house," Denise kept on, "and *see* that we're poor—see that all of us kids sleep in two bedrooms and you and Dad sleep on the living room sofa. And that the sofa is all torn—"

"Stop it! Stop it right there, Denise!" Mom demanded, as

she spoon-fed baby Jeanine. "*I* won't have any of that talk around this table. We're not poor at all. In fact, I think we're rich. It's all in how you look at things. Your nana says that if life gives you lemons, you just make lemonade. And I say we've got lots of lemonade around here!"

"Lemonade?" Denise sniffled, as the rest of us gobbled down our spaghetti.

"Yes, lemonade," Mom confirmed, looking around the table. "Do any of you ever go hungry?" We all shook our heads no. "And don't you have good clothes on your back?" We all looked down, not sure.

"Well"—Mom smiled—"you don't walk around naked, do you?"

"Barbara does in the back of Charlie's boat," Ellen chimed in.

"Do not."

"Do too."

"What matters," Mom interrupted, "is that if you look at what we've got, I say we've got a lot. We have each other. We laugh together, play together, help each other. I say we're rich."

"But, *Mom*!" Denise cried as if it would be her one and only chance for a boyfriend in her whole life. "Bruce is *really* good-looking and he dresses real nice. He's going to come in and see all the tape holding our sofas together."

Mom's face lit up with the birth of an idea. "After dinner," she announced, "we're all making some lemonade. Let's finish up—Ellen and Eddie clear the table, and everyone else report to the living room."

We gulped our dinner down, eager to see how Mom would make lemonade in the living room. "Sometimes," Mom instructed as she strategically sat each of her children on the two sofas, hiding the duct-taped rips, "things are better than they seem. All you have to do is see it that way! So, now see us as *rich*—and don't move! Don't move a muscle." Our arms and our legs were crisscrossed over one another in a homespun game of Twister, and the laughter became contagious. Mom had turned our ripped sofa into a giggling work of art.

When Denise welcomed her boyfriend into our living room, he didn't notice the rips on the sofas, because they didn't matter. What he saw instead was a family that he instantly liked. A family rich with the excitement of being a family.

Mom was right, I thought, looking anew at the reflection of my furry coat in the polished mahogany of my landlord's desk. *It's all in how you look at things.*

"Mr. Campagna!" I stated clearly. "I'm *not* a prostitute. I'm a *real estate broker*!"

Mr. Campagna put down his pen and hinted at a smile. "Well, if that's so, Miss Corcoran," he said, "why don't you just tell me how you're finding the real estate market?" I thought he might be testing me, so I told him about the success I was having at Mr. Giffuni's building, just three blocks away from his building. It was, of course, the only success I knew. When I told him I had gotten Mr. Giffuni $340 for his third-floor one-bedroom (not mentioning my wall idea), he seemed even more shocked than if I had been a prostitute.

I asked Mr. Campagna who rented his apartments, and he made it quite clear that "Mr. Herbert Cramer has always been the *exclusive* agent for all the Campagna properties." After he explained to me what an exclusive was and that it had a "guaranteed commission upon closing," I decided I had better try to get a few of those.

"Mr. Campagna," I asked, "if Mr. Cramer rents all your properties, why are there so many apartments vacant in our building?" He didn't seem to have an answer, so I suggested he give me just one of those apartments to rent. Not wanting to appear too pushy, I told him to give me the one Mr. Cramer liked the least.

Apartment 3C was next door to the superintendent's and had been vacant for a very long time. It had a narrow galley kitchen and a long, straight living room, with no hope of ever having a den. The apartment faced the back and never saw the light of day. Mr. Campagna's building at 86th Street and First Avenue was in the wrong location. It was just one block too east and one block too west, and the Gristedes grocery store directly across the street had tons of garbage stacked outside.

I arranged to meet my customers two blocks away on tony East End Avenue so I could begin each showing by admiring the wonderful prewar buildings that lined that street. "We're walking toward Fifth Avenue," I'd declare as we crossed First Avenue on East 86th Street. I'd gesture toward the Gristedes store "so conveniently located right across the street," and then whirl us through the revolving doors into Mr. O'Rourke's meticulously kept lobby. There I'd find Mr. O'Rourke (my new best salesman) proudly standing next to the mailboxes, and I'd introduce him to our prospective tenants.

He'd turn on his Irish charm and proudly take them on a tour of his spotless back service areas and stairwells. I'd thank Mr. O'Rourke and ride my customers up in the elevator, finishing my pitch with "The owner is so proud of this building that he moved his own family in!"

Once my customers saw all the good things Mr. Campagna's building had to offer, they were writing their checks before I even turned the keys of apartment 3C, apartment 7F, apartment 21A, and all the rest.

And that's how it came to be that Mr. Herbert Cramer no longer held the exclusive on Mr. Campagna's building.

I soon realized that if I hadn't almost been evicted as a

prostitute, I wouldn't have had the opportunity to meet my landlord and leave with a new apartment to rent. The eviction notice and its happy ending taught me that my mother was right—opportunity does hide in the worst situations. Finding opportunity is a matter of believing it's there.

4

Use Your Imagination
to Fill In the Blanks

1975. New York City.

"You want to *buy* an apartment?" I asked in disbelief as I left the Drake Hotel with a young engineer in the back of the cab. "*Buy*? Are you sure you don't mean *rent*?" My customer was hot to trot and was heading back to St. Louis the next night. He wanted to do so having bought a New York City apartment. I glanced down at the long, neatly typed list of rentals I had planned on showing him and knew I had to quickly fill in the blanks.

"No problem," I said as we crossed Lexington Avenue. "No problem at all."

I hadn't the faintest idea of how to *sell* apartments, but I knew if I let my hot potato out of the cab, he'd be sure to call another broker who actually had some apartments to sell. "Today will be a day of pure education," I began, pointing out the window. "We'll take a complete tour of *every* neighborhood in Manhattan so you'll know what each has to offer. I'll tell you everything good about each area as well as everything bad." I figured that would kill four hours. "It's important that you look at each neighborhood with an unbiased eye, so today we'll not even discuss prices." I said a quick prayer that the *New York Times* classifieds would at least give me a handle on what apartments might be selling for. The only way to find properties for sale was to hit the classifieds in search of owners advertising their own homes. It would be many years before the Multiple Listing Service, a computerized listing system giving all brokers instant access to every apartment available for sale, came to Manhattan.

"Once you've seen what's out there," I continued, "we'll find a quiet place to sit, and you can ask whatever questions you might have. If we're lucky, we should have time to squeeze in a bite to eat." I'd walk him six blocks to the Yorkville Diner and order the made-from-scratch souvlaki special. I figured that would swallow another hour and a half. If my math was correct, I would drop him back at the Drake around four, too late for him to take off with another broker.

"And tomorrow," I continued, "we'll start out bright and

early and look at all the apartments for sale in the neighbor-hoods you've selected. After today's tour, I'm sure you'll see them with a more knowledgeable eye."

I knew I had him in a New York minute. He nodded in dumb-founded agreement.

Although I didn't know a thing about the sales market, my buyer never doubted that I knew what I was talking about, because I had learned to fill in the blanks. It was a talent Mom taught me to recognize one night after dinner when I was in second grade, the day Sister Stella Marie told me I was stupid.

Second grade. Edgewater.

The night Sister Stella Marie ruined my day, I was painfully quiet while Mom rounded the table asking her usual "And how was your day?" Jump Johnny Jump announced that there was a new "cool" kid in the neighborhood and Tippy Toe Tommy reported that he had found a pair of red high heels in Mrs. Mertz's trash. When Mom got around to me, my eyes dropped to the turquoise tablecloth. "It was f-f-fine." I swallowed, not willing to tell my day's far-from-fine event.

That day after school, my second-grade teacher, Sister Ann Teresa, had told me to go to the first-grade classroom. I had walked down the hall to my old first-grade classroom, the Holy Rosary School classroom ruled by mean Sister Stella Marie, and I was petrified. I hesitantly pushed against the red metal door, and it opened on to a scene from every kid's worst nightmare. The only other kids in the room were Ellen Mulvaney (not her real name), known as "the retarded girl," and Rudy Valentino (really his name, but no relation to the famous 1920s actor. This Rudy lived in West New York, New Jersey), who spoke not a word of English. I looked at Ellen, then at Rudy, and my happy world screeched to a halt louder than fingernails on a blackboard. *Oh no*, I surmised, *I've been found out!*

Sister Stella Marie pointed her ruler at the desk between Ellen and Rudy. It was the same green ruler she had used to whack my neck in first grade whenever I couldn't figure out the answer to an arithmetic problem at the blackboard. I put my books on the metal rack under the seat and sat down. She pulled at her starched white collar, buried her hands in her draping black sleeves, and glowered. "You children can't read. And I'm going to teach you how."

While Sister read from the first-grade *Dick and Jane* reader, my mind immediately wandered down the hall and out of the building. Mr. Colontoni, our milkman (we called him Fat Ray Joe Potty Macaroni Colontoni), had given me an empty milk bottle that morning, and I had the bottle and a ball of yarn in the basket of my blue bike. I was going over to the Hudson River to catch a big fish. (Well, okay, a silver guppy. But magnified in the bottle, it would *look* like a big fish.) I was going to put it in a glass bowl, hide it under Ellen's bed, and keep it as a pet.

I was figuring out what I would feed my fish when Sister

Stella Marie barged into my daydream. "Well, Barbara Ann?" she asked. "Can you read the next page, please?"

Not wanting to admit I didn't know what page she was on, I told her, "No." Sister leaned over, close enough for me to see the black hairs twitching on her chin. "Barbara Ann, if you don't learn to pay attention," she scowled, "*you'll always be stupid.*"

I sucked in my breath, counted to a hundred, and concentrated hard so the tears burning my eyes wouldn't leak out. After class, I cried all the way back to our house on Undercliff Avenue, ran up to the woods, and sat on my big rock by the stream. I just knew I would *never* learn to read. Every time I guessed, I was wrong. And when I knew I was right, I was wrong. It wasn't that I wanted to daydream, it just always happened. I couldn't understand the words unless they were read to me: *b* always looked like *d*, *p* looked like *g*, and *e* just looked plain weird. When I tried to read, my brain was like our Christmas-tree lights that went out when one of the bulbs went bad.

I stifled my tears in time for dinner, not wanting anyone to know that Sister Stella Marie had said I was stupid. How could I be? I was the family entertainer, I created the games, and I was the director of all our basement Broadway shows! I *had* to be brilliant! I couldn't be stupid. *Could I?*

After the table was cleared, Mom asked me to stay with her in the kitchen. "I got a call today from Sister Stella Marie, Barbara Ann," she told me while sweeping the floor. "She said you're having trouble reading." My eyes welled with tears. Mom put down the broom, held my shoulders with both hands, and looked me straight in the eyes. "Barbara Ann," she said encouragingly, "don't you worry about it. You have a *wonderful imagination*. And with it, you can fill in *any* blanks."

She smiled and picked up her broom.

I knew I had to use my imagination to fill in the blanks for my customer the next day. Combing through the *Times* that evening in the new apartment I now shared with Ray, I realized that the New York market was changing. I had been so busy hustling rentals over the past two years, I hadn't noticed that the For Sale section of the paper had grown larger than the Rental section. More than half the classifieds formerly "for rent" were now advertised "for sale."

The whole town seemed to be going co-op. The city's long-standing rent control laws were strangling landlords' profits, pushing them to find new ways to make money. The answer was an "only in New York" harebrained scheme of selling apartments on a cooperative basis. This meant that co-op buyers didn't own their apartments outright, as with condominiums. Instead, they owned shares in the building corporation. Condos were the norm everywhere else in the world, but New York just had to be different.

I picked up my phone and called the first two-bedroom apartment I saw advertised by its owner—a RIV VU, 2 BR on

Sutton Place—and began what would become my standard sales pitch:

"Hello, this is Barbara Corcoran of Corcoran-Simone Real Estate. I'm working with a wonderful young engineer from Union Carbide who has been transferred to New York. He's in town for only one day and needs to buy an apartment tomorrow at the latest. He's asked me for an apartment with . . ." Then I read the seller the detailed description from his own ad, and he responded that his apartment sounded "just like that!"

"I know this might be a terrible imposition," I talked on, "but could I possibly show my customer your apartment at either nine fifteen or nine thirty tomorrow morning?"

After the seller agreed to the appointment, I bubbled him with thank-yous and ended the conversation with what would soon become my "Oh-and-by-the-way-just-one-more-question" Columbo-style close: a few last-second queries guaranteed to ferret out just how negotiable the price actually was.

"Oh, and by the way," I quickly asked the now excited seller, "have you had many offers on your apartment? Well, has it been on the market very long? Oh, really? Where will you be moving to? Oh, congratulations! And when are you expecting to close? Wonderful! I really look forward to seeing you tomorrow at nine fifteen." If the apartment turned out to be what my customer was actually looking for, I knew I was armed with enough information to close.

By the time I finished combing the paper that night and

working my sales pitch, I had twelve appointments set for the morning. Four were with nonnegotiable sellers, six with folks who would take something less than their price, and two were gotta-get-outta-here-fast desperate sellers.

God was my co-broker when my customer and I walked into the lobby of a twenty-story prewar on East 84th Street. Apartment 9K was our eighth apartment of the day, and as we walked past the doorman, my customer said, beaming, "My boss just bought in this building!" When I found out his boss was living three floors *below* Apartment 9K, all the rest was a piece of cake. The seller's moving boxes were packed in the living room, ready to go.

By the time I dropped my customer back off at the Drake, it was four o'clock. His flight was at seven. I circled back to the Hayman and Sumner stationery store, picked up a standard Blumberg sales contract, and rushed back to the tiny office Ray and I rented in a building on East 60th Street. I pecked out the needed information on my new IBM Selectric and circled back to the Drake. My customer was waiting out front. We jumped into a cab and headed to LaGuardia Airport.

The cab had reached the airport exit when my customer looked up from the contract I had handed him and asked the question that bedevils every real estate broker in New York: "Just what *is* a co-op, anyway?"

"It's what makes New York so special," I began, never having explained these details and having no idea how I would. "You'll be a sharecropper—I mean shareholder. That means the apartment is yours, but you don't really own it."

His eyebrow cocked slightly.

"Well, you own it, but you don't get a deed. Instead, you get a lease. But the great thing about a co-op lease is that there's absolutely no rent, just a monthly maintenance fee, which covers all the salaries of the super and the doormen. And the great thing about that is with a few hundred dollars at Christmas, they'll fix anything.

"And then there's the co-op's board of directors," I talked on, "a group of your neighbors whose job is to protect you."

His eyebrow relaxed.

"They decide what you can and can't do, can and can't change, and who you can and can't sell to, because that's what they're not paid to do. If you want to put in a dishwasher, they'll make sure it'll work by having the building's engineer review the plans your architect submits. He'll bill you by the hour and sometimes tell you that you can't do it."

His eyebrow climbed back up his forehead.

"But don't worry. As your boss probably knows already, you can pay the super to sneak one in; just make sure it's in a box that doesn't say 'dishwasher.'"

I could tell by the look on his face I needed to backpedal. "In short, a co-op is a one-of-a-kind thing and when you decide to sell the apartment, you have the right to sell it to whomever you want as long as all your neighbors like the person you want to sell it to. Your buyer will have to submit a list of all his personal assets, liabilities, and income to the board, just like you will now. And six full copies of his last three years' tax returns. You have all those things, right?"

His eyes glazed over, and I passed him my pen.

"Sign here."

5

Offer the Bigger Piece and Yours Will Taste Better

1976. Hackensack, New Jersey.

As it turns out, my boyfriend was never really Ramòne Simòne from the Basque Country. He was Ray Simon from West 185th Street.

I found this out when his development business went bust and we moved from the city apartment we shared into his mom's house, on Main Street in Hackensack. The house was vintage New Jersey, a two-story asbestos-sided colonial with a purple bathtub in the kitchen. Ray's mother, Vicki, doted on us. In the morning, she would strain our coffee through a white athletic sock and at night she'd cook us chicken and rice with black beans and plantains.

After dinner, I'd help her with her job of restringing pearls. Night after night, we cleared the dishes and Vicki covered the kitchen table with a dark terry-cloth towel. She would dump a sandwich bag full of pearls on the table, and we'd begin our three hours of work together. With a pair of small pointed scissors, I clipped the pearls from their original strand, washed them in a small bowl filled with soapy water, and rolled them dry on the towel. Next, I'd lay out the pearls in size order, the biggest in the middle, the smallest at the ends, and thread each pearl on a white silk string using a thin wire needle. I'd tie a knot tightly and evenly against each pearl, locking it into place, until I'd completed a perfect strand.

One night while stringing, Vicki explained how Ray had taken the name of her third husband, Mr. Simon.

"Mr. *Simon*?" I asked, an errant pearl hitting her linoleum with a *tink*. "I thought it was Simòne from the Basque Country."

"Oh, no, it was definitely Simon. He was from 185th Street and Amsterdam Avenue."

A few months later, Vicki gave her son a second chance as a developer by letting him put a second mortgage on her vintage colonial on Main Street.

Once Ray got back on his feet, his two oldest daughters

came to live with us. We had moved out of Vicki's house in Hackensack and into a new high-rise apartment in Fort Lee, not far from the old Fort Lee Diner. Every morning, I drove across the George Washington Bridge into Manhattan and each night I returned home in time to make dinner.

In my awkward new role as stepmom, I regularly sat at the dining room table helping Ray's daughters with their homework. His eleven-year-old, Laura, was having trouble reading, so I recounted the story of Sister Stella Marie and tried to do for her what my mom had done for me. "Laura, don't you worry about it," I told her. "You're a very hard worker, and that will get you through almost anything. Besides, you're so good with the big words, I bet one day you'll be a doctor!" Seeing her face light up made the many nights of doing homework worthwhile.

Ray rarely came into the Corcoran-Simone office anymore, other than to sign checks. He was working late more frequently, often meeting with his carpenters, plumbers, and electricians. But he always got home in time to kiss his girls good night. One Tuesday, Ray came home at six thirty, and I was surprised to see him home so early. I was in the kitchen pulling the spaghetti off the stove.

"I have something serious I need to speak with you about," he told me.

"Sure," I said, preparing to dump the spaghetti into a colander. "What's up?"

"I'm going to marry Tina," he said.

My hands went limp, and I sloshed the spaghetti into the sink. "*Tina*? My *secretary*?" I stammered. "I-I don't understand."

He shifted his weight and put his hands in his pockets. "I guess you should start looking for an apartment or something," he continued. "But take your time."

"It'll take five minutes!" was all I could muster.

The next morning, I couldn't lift my head, and my feet couldn't make it onto the small rug beside my friend Catherine's sofa. I was too proud to call my mom and tell her she'd been right about Ray all along. For the first time in my life, I called in sick.

I questioned my worth without Ray and traced over the details of our last year together, searching for the signs that should have given me an idea of what was going on. I was filled with anger. I hated Tina, and I hated Ray, too. But most of all I hated me for being the fool.

Two days later, Catherine came over to the sofa with her home remedy for puffy eyes. "Now, Barbara," she began, as I lay mummified on her quilted sofa, "today is the day you're going back to work!" She put two soggy tea bags on my eyes and made a feeble attempt at a pep talk, intermittently spooning warm water onto the tea bags. An hour later, I stumbled to the shower, and for the first time in days, looked in the mirror. I looked just like a raccoon.

"Catherine?" I yelped. "What kind of tea was that?"

There was a long silence in the living room. "Oh my God!" she finally yelled back. "It's Bigelow blackberry!"

Six coats of Maybelline Cover Stick and a whole lot of coaxing later, I put on a please-don't-notice-me beige outfit—beige blouse, beige pants, and matching beige shoes—and walked to my office on East 60th Street.

I hesitantly stepped off the elevator, sucked in a long, slow breath, and marched into the sea of fourteen sales desks and salespeople facing me at the door. Everyone looked up. I had no idea what they did or didn't know, so I smiled my best smile and made a beeline for my office. "Good morning, Norma! Hello, Esther!" I waved as my eyes worked hard to avoid Tina's desk. That's when I lost connection with my legs, and I tripped— no, flopped—onto the floor, a sprawled blur of embarrassed beige.

Of course, Tina got to me first. "Are you okay, Barbara?" Ray's fiancée kindly asked. "You look like you're hurt."

I knew my mother's red blotches were forming on my chest and was grateful for my beige turtleneck. "I'm fine," I stammered, groping for the contents of my purse. "I'm fine!" I grabbed for my subway tokens and tampons as they rolled to the far reaches. "My purse is fine, I'm fine, *everything's just fine!*"

A phone rang, providing the needed distraction for me to limp into the office I shared with Ray. He was sitting at his desk smiling.

"Tina can't work here anymore," I announced.

"Tina's staying," Ray informed me. "Remember, Barbara, I'm the majority partner here. I own 51 percent of this business, and that puts me in control."

Our romance had died a sudden death, but it would be a long time before we broke up the business. Somehow, I plowed through the next year and a half of entrances and smiles, while slowly building the courage to walk away from Ray for good. One Thursday afternoon, as we made our weekly deposit at the bank, it hit me—now was the time and I had the courage to do it.

"Ray," I said, "I'm going to start my own company."

His left eye twitched behind his blue aviator shades, but he remained calm. "You might want to give that a little more thought," he suggested.

So I did. Overnight. And what I thought was this: *I actually know what I'm doing and I can do it without him.* But how to leave him gracefully had me stumped.

Lying in bed that night, I decided to suggest we divide the business the way my mom did her cake.

Sunday night. Edgewater.

Mom made our favorite dessert on Sunday nights, a Duncan Hines Devil's Food Cake in her rectangular aluminum pan. After dinner, she placed the warm cake on top of a waffle-weave dish towel in the middle of the table, and we all watched and drooled as she cut it into twelve pieces using the edge of her spatula. As we went around the table, each child eyed and vied for the biggest piece.

When there were only two pieces left, it was Eddie's turn to pick, and he reached for the bigger of the two. "Eddie!" Mom interrupted. "Let your sister Ellen go first."

Mom had a rule that when there were two pieces left of anything, we had to offer the bigger piece to the other person. She insisted it made your piece taste better.

Ellen, who was toiling away at the dishes in the sink like the Good Housekeeping Seal come to life, wiped her hands, marched over to the table, and picked exactly the piece Eddie wanted.

"Don't worry, Eddie," Mom reminded him, "now *yours* will taste even better!"

That's it! I concluded. *I've got to offer Ray the "bigger piece."* I turned off the light and went to sleep.

Ray was spending a lot more time at the office, and when he arrived the next afternoon, I was ready for him.

"There's something serious I need to talk to you about, Ray," I said as he settled into his black leather chair. "I've given things a lot of thought just as you suggested, and I *am* going to open my own business." I waited, but he said nothing. "So, we have to decide how to divide up the company. We'll need to establish two separate bank accounts and split our receivables and cash. One of us can keep this office, but one of us will have to move. And we'll each need our own phone number."

Ray sat silent.

"Since we have fourteen salespeople, we can each take seven. I suggest we do a football-type draw, and since you're the majority shareholder, you should get to pick first." Ray seemed pleased with the "you pick first" terms. I had already reviewed the list of salespeople and knew I needed Esther to help me move my business forward. For me, Esther was indispensable. I figured if I went first and picked her, Ray might argue to get her.

"Okay," he began. "I'll take Norma." Norma was clearly the big moneymaker. She was our top-producing salesperson, and her sales alone accounted for 60 percent of our company's commissions. And now Norma and her 60 percent were Ray's.

"Okay, then," I said, "I'll take Esther." Esther wasn't our top moneymaker, but she was a consistent producer and had all the traits I needed to build my new business. Esther was smart, organized, and loyal, and she worked twice as hard as everyone else.

We went back and forth until we had divided up the remaining dozen salespeople.

"I'll keep the main 355-1200 phone number," Ray declared. Ray always said ours was a "very important number" and made the company sound big.

"Then I'll get a new number," I agreed. I knew Ray would think 355-3550 sounded less important, but I thought it was snappy and far easier to remember.

"And I'll stay in this office," Ray concluded, "and *you'll* have to move." I nodded. Although it would be expensive to move, I knew it would be a fresh start. The same space was available three floors higher with a lot more light, and I already knew I could rent it for the same amount of money.

Once we finished all our business, I put my calendar into my shoulder bag and zipped it up. "What will you call your company, Ray?" I asked, standing near the door.

"Pogue-Simone, of course!" he bragged. *How romantic*, I thought painfully, but quickly comforted myself with the thought that people would have a hard time spelling or pronouncing Tina's last name anyway.

"Well, Ray," I announced, "I'm going to call *my* new company *The Corcoran Group*." As I said it, I knew it sounded right.

We shook hands for the last time. Ray was obviously pleased with the results and was relishing what he viewed as a clear win for himself through and through. He got up, walked past me, and then turned around. "You know, Barb," he said, putting his hands in his pockets, *"you'll never succeed without me."* And with that, Ramòne Simòne strutted away.

I leaned back on my old desk, the one Ray had just picked for Tina, and vowed to myself that I would rather *die* than let him see me fail!

6

Put the Socks in the
Sock Drawer

1978. The Corcoran Group. Three days before opening.

"*No!*" I shrieked as I opened the door into a forest of six-foot cartons. I squeezed through the cardboard hulks, waded through a sea of spilled manila folders, and picked up a handful of scattered Bic pens. Gawking at the pyramid of tangled chair legs that the Nice Jewish Boy Movers had piled in the middle of my spanking-new office, I worried aloud, "How the heck am I going to pull this off?"

I had rented an office three flights above the offices of Pogue-Simone, leaving the kelly green walls, dented black desks, and makeup-smeared phones for Tina and Ray. Instead of buying furniture and equipment, I had decided to lease new phones, typewriters, and desks, to stretch my $14,837 half of the Corcoran-Simone money as far as it would go. I splurged an extra eleven bucks a month for charcoal gray desks instead of the standard-issue black ones, and paid the super a little extra to paint the walls a fancy cranberry rather than the usual institutional white.

Trying to swallow my anxiety along with my breakfast, I looked back at the door and thought, *I just don't have enough time, money, or help, and in three days I'm going to have a whole lot of salespeople with a whole lot of needs walking right through that door!*

For the first time in my life, I felt really alone. I put my coffee aside and thought about calling my mom, but I didn't. Ever since I'd left home with Ray against her wishes, I had been determined not to need her anymore.

I looked at my watch. It was six thirty A.M. Mom would be beginning her morning routine about now. I could see her running through the house putting everything in order, and I wished she could be here with me to whip everything into shape. I knew my mother would know exactly what to do.

School day. Edgewater.

"Good morning, everyone!" Mom's voice boomed as she ripped the covers from each of our beds. Dazed, I made my way to the kitchen table, took a cereal bowl from the stack, and stumbled to the stove for my one scoop of hot Quaker Oats.

"Good morning, Mom," I mumbled.

"Good morning, Barbara Ann," she said back, smiling.

I sat down as I always did in my assigned seat next to the bathroom door, and stirred milk and brown sugar into my oatmeal as it cooled. My brothers and sisters were all doing the same. At seven A.M. sharp, when I had only three spoonfuls to go, Mom declared breakfast over. We had twenty minutes to wait in line for the bathroom to brush our teeth and comb our hair, and two minutes more to put on the clothes Mom had placed at the foot of our beds.

"Where's my socks?" Eddie yelled to no one.

"Where's my socks?" was a question you asked only once in our house. Every sock in our house was stored in the two square drawers on the wall between the bathroom and the stove. The top drawer was filled with the girls' white nylon socks, and the bottom with the boys' navy cotton socks.

Mom pulled Eddie by his ear into the kitchen, opened the bottom sock drawer, and pointed. "Socks," she pronounced slowly and with emphasis, "are *always* in the sock drawer." She left Eddie rubbing his ear and darted off to sort the laundry.

My mother had a routine for everything. When she sorted the laundry, she started by dumping it all in the middle of the living room floor. Then she divided it into the white pile and the color pile, and subdivided those into heavy and light fabrics.

Next, she placed the four piles atop four dirty bedsheets, tied a knot in each, and slung them two-to-a-shoulder into the kitchen. By day's end, Mom had sorted, washed, hung, folded, and put away eight loads of laundry.

She prepared for school mornings the night before, painting our white bucks shoes on top of the living room radiator with Kiwi shoe polish and her Sherwin-Williams paintbrush. Early on, she had painted the radiator white so her late-night drips wouldn't show.

Then Mom made our lunches in less than two minutes. First, she plopped a tub of Skippy peanut butter, a jar of Welch's grape jelly, and a five-pound bag of McIntosh apples on the kitchen table. She dealt out twenty slices of Wonder Bread into two perfectly parallel rows and, with her ten-inch icing knife, spread the top row with peanut butter and the bottom row with jelly. Then she flipped the top slices onto the bottoms, halved each sandwich on the diagonal, and wrapped each in waxed paper. After punching open ten brown paper bags, Mom dropped a sandwich and an apple inside. At noon the next day, we opened our lunch bags to find one apple and a concave peanut butter and jelly on white.

"C'mon, c'mon!" Mom yelled to us every morning at 7:20 as she stood by the door guarding our white bucks warming in size order beneath the radiator. "Hurry or you're going to be late!"

We slid in our socked feet across the turquoise tile of the living room, dropped into our white bucks, grabbed a lunch bag, and headed out the door.

———

After thinking about the systems that made my mother's house work, I knew the only chance I had of having a well-run office rested on having a place and a system for everything. So, I spent the weekend planning and getting organized.

First, I made a list of everything that *hadn't* worked at the old office, a long list of time wasters, and figured out how to eliminate them. Then I made a list of what *had* worked and devised ways to do them even better. I thought through my salespeople's office needs, numbered the most important ones, and crossed out the ones that could wait. I tore the lists from my yellow legal pad and hailed a cab over to Hayman and Sumner stationers. I browsed through the merchandise, sizing up its usefulness, and headed back to the office with a large carton full of file folders, colored index cards, and labels.

9:15 A.M. *The Corcoran Group. First day.*

"Good morning," I said as each of my seven salespeople cautiously walked through the door. "After you hang your coat, please come over here, reach in, and pull out a number." I had put in a number for every desk and folded the fourteen pieces of paper and put them in a red Bloomingdale's shopping bag. Each number corresponded with a number I had taped to the desks.

Cathy picked first, tentatively reaching into the bag and pulling out a number. "Oh, Cathy!" I exclaimed. "Congratulations! You got number seven! You picked the *best* desk here!" David was next and pulled out number three. "Is that number three you have there, David?" I gushed. "Congratulations, David! *You* picked the best desk here."

The number I was pulling had everyone laughing.

"Now, remember," I shouted into the excited sales area, "if you don't like your desk, don't even give it a moment's thought, because we'll be changing all our seats in six months anyway! And if you do like your desk, don't get too used to it, because we'll be changing all our seats in six months anyway! And please don't put your things on the empty desk next to yours, because I'll be filling that seat in no time at all."

I had placed a small yellow rose in a white vase with a hand-written note on each desk. The salespeople smiled as they read it: "I'm so happy you're here! xoxo—Barb."

I spotted John Bachman about to post his cardboard DO NOT DISTURB sign high above desk number five. From his perfectly parted blond hair to his stiff ironing-board walk, everything about John said "Leave me alone."

I approached him cautiously. "John?" I interrupted. "You may have needed that 'do not disturb' sign in our old office, but you won't need it around here. In this office, *everyone* can disturb *everyone.*"

John twisted his pinky ring a half turn to the right and said with a nod, "Vell, if zat's vat you vant . . ." and put away his sign.

I walked to the front of the office and shouted to get everyone's attention, "Okay, now, please get yourself a cup of coffee and a doughnut, and we'll start our meeting." While they
sugared, milked, and stirred, I began. "Good morning once
again, everyone!"

Everyone humored me and chimed back, "Good morning,
Barbara."

"Today, I have six announcements to make. The first is that
we're going to have breakfast here together every Monday
morning. It will begin promptly at nine thirty and end exactly at
ten fifteen.

"The second announcement is that we'll be starting a
brand-new system for our listing information, and here's how it
will work." I held up four different-colored index cards. "The
new listing cards will carry the same property information as our
old ones did, but the new colors will make it easier for you to
find the right-size apartment when you need it." I demonstrated
each color as I spoke. "All studio apartment information will be
written on the white cards, all one-bedrooms on the yellow
cards, two-bedrooms on blue, and three-bedrooms and larger
will always be on pink. Every time you get a new listing, you'll
write it on the appropriate colored card and file it in the corre-
sponding colored box. As our new colored listing system will
help everyone, no one will receive listing credit if the apartment
is written on the wrong-colored card. Do you understand?"

I smiled and nodded, and everyone nodded along.

"The third announcement is about getting better property information. I'm sure you all agree that the more we know about each property for sale, the better chance we have of selling it. So, from now on, I'll be paying cash for better information. For example, when David writes up all the details about his new listing, and Sandy, after seeing it, is able to add one more fact to David's information, I'll give Sandy one dollar for helping David." I waved a fistful of dollars in the air and smiled.

Everyone smiled back.

"Announcement four is about the new commission form you'll need to complete if you want to get paid." I held up the familiar eight-by-eleven sheet of paper. "Well, now the commission request form is green and it also has a back side." I flipped it over, showing the list of questions I had worked hours to create. "When you answer the questions on the back, we'll all have a much better idea of where our business is actually coming from and what is working and what is not.

"For example, where did you get your customer? Did they call you on a Sunday ad? Find you in an open house? Or were they referred by a friend or business associate? Simply check a box. Where is your customer living now? Is he here in the city? Or is he moving from another state? Another country? Check a box. And what business is your customer in? Is he married? Single? Children? How old is he? Simply check a box. Knowing where our business is coming from will help us all get more business."

Everyone nodded along with me.

"If we know more about our sellers and how each deal was made," I continued, "we'll all become much better negotiators. So some of the other questions are about the transaction itself. How long was the property on the market before it sold? What was the first offer? And how much did the seller negotiate before the deal was done?

"The new commission form will take only three minutes to complete. All you have to do is check the appropriate boxes. Commissions will be paid every Friday, and no commission will be paid without it."

Everyone nodded. So I went on: "Do you remember back at the old office when we desperately looked for floor plans while our customers waited in the lobby? Do you remember the day we actually dumped out John's drawer looking for the floor plan of his new listing at Two Sutton Place? Well, after today, we're never going to search for a lost floor plan again. Because now, when you get a floor plan for your new listing, you'll immediately create a floor plan folder for *everyone* to use."

I stood and waved a sample folder for everyone to see, and demonstrated. "First, you'll staple the new floor plan to the inside of a manila folder and print the address boldly on the folder's tab." I walked over to the copy machine, placed the file facedown, and pressed the Print button. "Next, you'll make ten copies of the original and put them all inside the folder. Then you place the floor plan file by street order in the new floor plan drawer at the front of the office. And if you take the last copy from the folder, you're the one responsible for using the stapled original to make ten more copies to put inside the folder." As the copy machine finished, I said, "Ta-dah! No more lost floor plans."

Everyone applauded.

"And this brings us to our last announcement today, the Good Idea Box." I pulled out a cardboard shoe box on which I had drawn a giant yellow lightbulb. "This box is for *good ideas*," I enunciated. "Whenever you have a new idea, I'd like to know about it. I don't care if it's a big idea, small idea, or even a stupid idea—all ideas are welcome! I'll pay five dollars for every idea, and I'll even give five bucks for a complaint—but only if it's accompanied by a solution. So, here's the first five bucks for John Bachman, who suggested only ten minutes ago that we eliminate the 'do not disturb' signs from the office. Great job, John!" I said, and placed the money in his limp hand.

I looked around the room and asked, "So, does anyone have any questions?"

Seven dazed salespeople shook their heads no.

"Okay, then, that's everything. The Monday meeting is now over."

The phone rang, and I reached over the reception desk and happily answered, "Good morning, The Corcoran Group."

7

If There's More Than One Kid to Wash, Set Up a Bathtime Routine

Second week. The Corcoran Group.

"'Seven salespeople needed. . . .'" I read the words of my help wanted ad to the phone operator at the *New York Times* and realized it sounded desperate. "Wow," I said, "when I read it out loud, 'needed' sounds really *needy*, don't you think?" The operator said nothing. "Let me change that to 'Seven desks are awaiting.'" I heard her fingers typing. "Is 'awaiting' a word?" I asked. She said nothing. I looked down at the many versions of the ad I had scratched out on my pad and figured I'd better rethink my approach. "You know what? Let me think a little more about this and call you back."

I had two problems to solve. First, I had to attract enough applicants to give me the best chance of finding good hires. Second, I knew if potential salespeople saw us as we were, desperate to fill our extra seven desks, they would surely shy away! I knew I needed a way to make the good candidates out there want us.

Saturday night. Edgewater. The front steps.

"Who wants to go to the Dairy Queen?" Dad asked us as we gathered on our front steps.

"Me! Me! Me!" we all chimed in unison, raising our hands.

"Who wants to get an icy cold chocolate Dilly Bar?" Dad continued. "Or maybe an extra-thick frozen strawberry shake in a big white cup with a straw to suck it all up?"

"Me! Me! I would, Dad!" every voice begged.

"Or maybe," he tempted further, "a double banana split with three big scoops of chocolate, butter pecan, and strawberry ice cream, all covered with caramel syrup and a big pile of whipped cream?"

"Me! Dad, me! I would!" we all chimed back. Denise jumped up, John pushed Tommy aside so his hand could be better seen, and Ellen clambered onto Dad's lap.

Dad had our attention, and we waited with drooling mouths for his next words.

"Well, kids," Dad said with a smile, putting his arms around

Ellen and me, "so would I. Yep, that sure would be nice, but . . . not tonight, kids. Maybe next week."

Denise sat down, John dropped his hand, and Ellen slumped against Dad's chest.

The next Saturday, though, Dad would end his tease with, "Well then, get in the car, kids. We're going to Dairy Queen!" And the chocolate Dilly Bar I ordered was even sweeter because we'd been made to want it even more.

Thinking back on Dad's Dairy Queen tease, I redialed the *New York Times*.

"Hello, are you the same operator I was just speaking to?" I asked the voice on the other end of the line. "Oh, well, anyway, I'd like to place a help wanted ad in this Sunday's paper." And I read:

Sales, Real Estate

ONE EMPTY DESK

Only one desk available for a positive, high-energy person wishing to earn large commissions. Exceptional company. No experience necessary.

The Corcoran Group. 212-355-3550

I knew the ad would work.

I opened my calendar and cleared my Monday schedule.

Now to deal with the next problem. When the phone started ringing, I was going to need one heck of a routine to take all the calls, interview all the salespeople, and hire the right ones.

Bathtime. The Corcoran kitchen.

"Thank you, God," Mom prayed every night as she soaked in the hot water of what she called the "holiest tub in Edgewater." "Thank you for giving me three minutes for myself." Exactly two minutes and fifty-eight seconds later, Mom jumped out of the tub, threw on her pink robe, and took two broad strides out of the bathroom and into the kitchen. She was ready for the bathtime routine.

She punched the Talk button on the black wall intercom that Uncle Alan had borrowed from his job at Bell Telephone. "Kids!" her voice squawked, as it did every night on our bedroom speaker. "You have exactly five minutes to finish your homework and report to the kitchen! I repeat, *five* minutes. And, Eddie, leave Johnny alone!"

We all collected in the kitchen and took our place in line by the kitchen sink. Eight-year-old Denise, the oldest, then me, then Eddie, then Ellen, and then Johnny holding little Tommy's hand.

Dad was in charge of washing each kid and Mom was in charge of rinsing. First up was Denise, who climbed onto the counter next to the white porcelain double sink. Dad slid her into the deep side of the sink filled to the brim with warm sudsy water. Starting with her head, he kneaded the shampoo through her hair, down her back, over her behind, past her legs, and finally between her toes.

When Denise stepped over into the clear water of Mom's rinsing sink, Dad slid me from the counter into the washing sink and began the same routine. Mom used her black-handled aluminum pot to give Denise a final rinse, and then, like a baton in a relay, quickly passed Denise back off to Dad for drying.

I stepped over into Mom's rinsing sink, and on cue my brother Eddie stepped into the washing sink, where he waited while Dad sat Denise on top of the terry-covered counter and used a big towel to speed-dry her hair. Denise's job was to press her head into Dad's chest as hard as she could and try to hum "*Aaaaaah*" straight through the vibration to the very end.

Mom had our flannel pajamas on the kitchen table waiting in size order. As I was *aaaaaah*-ing through the speed-dry, Eddie was getting Mom's final rinse, Ellen was stepping into Dad's sink, and Johnny and Tommy were waiting in line.

By the time the calls started coming in on Sunday morning, I had set up a routine as squeaky clean as Mom's to move the sales applicants in and out of the office.

"Hello," the first caller pleasantly began, "I'm calling about your empty desk advertisement in today's paper."

Our new receptionist responded with my carefully worded script: "Thank you for calling. If you would hold just a moment, I'll connect you with the president of our company."

As I picked up the phone, the applicant politely repeated, "I'm calling about your empty desk ad in today's paper."

"Oh, thank you for calling," I responded, "but unfortunately that position has already been filled."

"What?" the caller asked with surprise. "How could that be? It just appeared in this morning's paper!"

"Yes, and I'm very sorry," I explained sympathetically. "But we usually have a long list of people waiting to join our company, and the positions are often taken before the ad even appears. I'm really sorry to disappoint you."

"Well . . . okay," the caller said, "I understand—"

"But," I interrupted, "new positions do open up from time to time, and I'd be happy to get together with you anyway. Then at least we'd have a chance to meet one another so when another position opens, I could call you immediately."

"Oh, would you? That would be so nice of you."

"How about tomorrow at ten?" I asked.

I narrowed twenty-seven would-be salespeople into sixteen appointments and scheduled them all for the next day between ten A.M. and one P.M. Each applicant was surprised to find three other people already waiting, and jockeyed for a piece of the bench at the front of the office.

Our receptionist greeted everyone with a very important-looking four-page sales application. Per my instructions, she gave those who appeared well groomed and well dressed a pen. And those applicants who weren't dressed for success she handed a pencil. This way, when the applicants called to follow up later, I had a surefire way to tell which callers to spend my time with.

I scanned the sales applications to ferret out the applicants' personal references and home address, because that information would tell me whether they already had the contacts and customer leads I knew I couldn't give them.

The first interview of the day was with a well-coiffed woman in her early forties. After chatting at length about her children, hobbies, and husbands, I corralled the conversation back in with, "Mary, I'm so happy you've spent all this time telling me about your family and friends." I smiled and she smiled back. "But would you mind if I'm totally honest with you?"

"Please, of course not," she invited.

"Well, Mary, after working with so many different people, I guess I've concluded that great salespeople have a few things in common. The first is empathy. You know, the ability to get along with people. And, Mary, it's obvious to me that you're very, very good with people. Would you agree?"

Mary straightened her back, sat up proudly, and agreed. "Yes, of course. Yes, yes, I'm *very* good with people."

I smiled and then paused with obvious concern. "But," I continued in a more serious voice, "I've also found that the other thing all great salespeople share is a real need to succeed—I'd almost call it a killer instinct. And for whatever reason, I'm just not getting that from you." Then I sat back in my chair and waited for her response.

For the next five minutes, Mary gave a long dissertation on how she really *was* aggressive. Her words were right, but I knew her music was all wrong. So, I bade her good-bye and promised to call if a position became available. I knew it never would.

The next applicant sashayed in with her black alligator brief-case, removed an alligator glove, and extended her manicured hand across my desk. She explained she had "four years' real estate experience" and knew all the right people in all the right places. In three short minutes, she made it perfectly clear to me she had nothing to learn. And I believed her and sent her on her way.

Thirteen applicants later, a tall, thin woman named Emily O'Sullivan marched confidently into my office and plopped herself down. She wore a hot-pink tweed suit trimmed with a contrasting taupe braid. Her suit had more buttons than I had in my whole wardrobe. They were bright gold with two raised Cs on each of them. I immediately made a mental note to imitate their design for my new Corcoran Group logo.

When I got to my standard "I don't think you're aggressive" line, Emily was so insulted I thought she'd leap across the desk and grab my throat. And as she yap-yap-yapped in my face, I knew Emily was the right gal for me.

8

If You Want to Be in Two Places at Once, Borrow a Reel-to-Reel

Sixth month. The Corcoran Group.

My "empty desk" ad produced more people to start, train, and motivate than I had time to start, train, and motivate.

Each morning, I hit the phones at eight thirty sharp to finish setting up my sales appointments for the day. I was ready by nine forty-five, when my eager new hurdle jumpers showed up for their sales training.

We spent the first twenty minutes reviewing our customer cards and dividing them into three piles based on how urgently each customer needed a place to live. The hot-to-trot customers formed the "A" pile, the I'll-buy-it-when-I-find-its were labeled "B"s, and the "C" rating was reserved for the annoying I'll-shop-till-I-drop group of time wasters. I had each salesperson tear up their "C" customers and toss them in the trash.

For the next forty-five minutes, we called each of our new property listings, asking questions like "When are you moving? Why? When do you need to close?" Then we would rate each seller from least to most motivated and divide them into three piles, labeling them "not negotiable," "will take something less," and "gotta get outta here fast!"

I worked with my bright-eyed crew until eleven A.M., took a minute to tell them how much I appreciated them, and darted out for my afternoon apartment showings. Around six thirty P.M., I rushed back to the office to return phone calls and set up my sales appointments for the next morning. Then, as it was the days before cell phones and e-mails, I read through the numerous notes left for me in my in-box and jotted my responses to the salespeople.

By eight o'clock, I locked the door and walked the eleven blocks home to my one-bedroom floor-through on East 69th Street. I climbed the stairs to the second floor, turned the double deadbolt lock, took a consoling breath, and opened the door into the only place I had ever lived by myself in my life. I was thankful to be too busy and too exhausted to feel lonely.

I realized that in trying to be everything to everybody at my fledgling company, I was only fooling myself. I knew I couldn't keep up my exhausting routine much longer. I knew I needed to find another me.

Bedtime. The girls' room.

"Eddie!" Mom hollered to Dad. "Eddie, they're ready!"

As the household population grew, Mom started running out of time. In order to give herself the needed minutes each night to prepare for the mornings, she was (thankfully) forced to give up her position as one of our two rooms' nightly lullaby singers. She had Dad record his favorite songs on a brown reel-to-reel tape deck that Uncle Alan had borrowed from his job at Bell Telephone. Then she set up Dad to alternate nights between the girls' room and the boys' room, singing us songs to lull us to sleep. The room that wasn't getting Dad's live performance could instead listen to *Dad's Greatest Hits* on the reel-to-reel. In so doing, Mom succeeded in putting Dad in two places at once and creating a stand-in for her.

Tonight, Dad was live in the girls' room. He sauntered in with his old wood guitar and sat down on the edge of Ellen's bed. I watched as he carefully removed his pick from between the E, G, and A strings and strummed a single sweet C chord. Denise blurted out the first request: "Sing us the one about 'Heart of My Heart,' Dad!"

"And 'Valla-Valla-Vee Was in the Army,'" Ellen quickly added, as she sat upright in her bed.

"And what about you, Barbara Ann?" Dad asked. "What will it be tonight?"

I always waited so I could hear Dad say my name. "My usual," I replied. "Sing 'Give My Regards to Hoboken.'"

Dad began singing in his Perry Como voice. I scrunched the covers up tight against my chin, stretched my toes as far as I could, and fought my heavy eyelids until I heard the very last words of my favorite song.

> Give my regards to Hoboken,
> Down where the breezes blow.
> In all kinds of weather,
> You'll find us together,
> In H-O-B-O-K-E-N, E-N,
> In H-O-B-O-K-E-N!

While Dad crooned in the girls' room and his voice reel-to-reeled in the boys' room, Mom made the next day's lunches in the kitchen.

The day Esther Kaplan had arrived for her interview back at the old Corcoran-Simone office, she'd worn a two-piece knit dress that was mostly cream and green with small touches of cranberry. She was a small-framed, elegant woman in her mid-forties and carried a beige handbag with a Bakelite handle and clasp.

She explained that she was an executive secretary to a real estate attorney and wanted to make a change in her career.

The first thing Esther did was present her card, which she carefully removed from her purse, allowing me a quick glimpse inside.

Esther's handbag was a small miracle of organization, a miniature file cabinet disguised as a fashion accessory. She unzipped one of the two interior pockets, extracted her card, handed it to me, zipped the pocket, and snapped the clasp. Before the interview was over, I knew I'd feel safe with my wallet in Esther Kaplan's purse.

That's what I remembered as I now desperately needed someone to help me run my new office. And after working side by side with Esther for the past two years, I knew I could trust her with any amount of responsibility, if she would only agree to take it on. So one night I asked her if she could stay an hour late.

"Esther," I began, "I really appreciate your taking the time out of your busy day to meet with me, and I must say that I'm constantly amazed at what a phenomenal salesperson you've become. I remember you made your first sale your very first month at Corcoran-Simone, and I think you've made a sale every month since. I frankly don't know how you do it. Esther, you are truly an amazing lady." I meant what I said and hoped Esther knew it.

"Well, thank you, Barb," Esther quietly replied. "That's very nice to hear."

"Esther, here's why I wanted to talk with you tonight. I'm wondering if you would consider taking on more of a leadership role here at the company," I continued.

Esther raised a cautious brow. "What leadership role would that be?" she asked.

"Why, the most important position there is, *vice president* of The Corcoran Group," I heralded.

"And what would the vice president of The Corcoran Group do?" she inquired.

"Basically, you would be an extension of me," I explained. "When I'm out showing apartments, you would act with my full authority here at the office. And when you were out showing apartments, I would act in your stead. I guess you could say we'd be like one person, and together we would build the business."

"Well, Barb, I don't really know what to say," Esther answered, obviously flattered and surprised. "I'll have to give this some serious consideration." She hesitated, clutching her purse a bit closer to her chest. "May I ask what the position would pay?"

I hadn't really thought about this minor point, but suddenly, Wimpy from the Popeye cartoons popped into my head.

"I would gladly pay you Tuesday for one hamburger today," I joked.

Esther straightened in her chair, tilted her head, and said, "I'm not quite sure I understand."

I laughed. "Esther, I don't have any money to offer you right now, but this is more important than money. I'm offering you a *partnership*, and I could pay you later in stock. In fact, I'll pay you 10 percent of my company stock in three years, if you help me build my business today." With that, I took a yellow legal pad from the shelf and drew three wide columns across the top.

The first I labeled "Year." The second, "# of Salespeople." And the last column I labeled "Commissions." I figured my fourteen salespeople would bring in $250,000 this year, so in the first row, I wrote "1978," "14," and "$250,000." Then as Esther watched with interest, I quickly worked down each column, doubling the number of salespeople and commissions on each year as I went.

YEAR	# OF SALESPEOPLE	COMMISSIONS
1978	14	$250,000
1979	28	$500,000
1980	56	$1,000,000
1981	112	$2,000,000
1982	224	$4,000,000
1983	448	$8,000,000
1984	896	$16,000,000
1985	1,792	$32,000,000!!!!!

"Thirty-two million dollars!" I exclaimed when I completed the last row. The number astonished even me. I was amazed to see how easy it would be to become rich! I looked up at Esther,

circled the impressive sum, and gushed, "Well, Esther, what do you think?"

I don't know if Esther believed me or not, but she bought in, deferring her salary in the first few years in exchange for her partnership interest. The next day, while Esther was running the office, I was buzzing about town, hustling hard for our $32 million.

9

It's Your Game;
Make Up Your Own Rules

1981. Suffern, New York.

I opened the *New York Times* and read the headline:

NEW YORK REAL ESTATE MARKET
SHOWS SIGNS OF LEVELING OFF

"According to Brewster Ives," the article read, "chairman of the Douglas Elliman–Gibbons & Ives real estate company, Manhattan home prices have dipped for the first time since 1973. . . ."

"Blah, blah, blah . . ." I said to myself as I scratched out my competitor's name in the *New York Times* with my black marker.

"Why is that guy always quoted in the paper and I'm not?" I complained to the handsome guy seated next to me at the industry gathering at the Holiday Inn in Suffern, New York.

"You probably need a PR company," he said, grinning.

"What's that?" I asked.

"A public relations company," he said, extending his big hand. "Hi, I'm Bill Higgins from Higgins Realtors in New Jersey. We're the oldest and boldest real estate company in the state, and I suppose you're the new broker from the city?" He didn't wait for a response. "I heard this PR guy speak at a conference last month in Boston, named Solomon—Steve Solomon. He's from Manhattan and that's what he does, gets people in the paper. You should look him up. He got my name on the front page of the *Bergen Record*," he bragged. "Yep, right under Nancy Reagan's!"

My immediate reaction was *Who is this guy? And what is he talking about?* But when I got back to the city, I called Steve Solomon and made an appointment. The game of PR was about to begin.

"You charge seven hundred and fifty dollars *a month*? Every month?" I asked Mr. Solomon in disbelief, whisking my bangs away from my eyes. "That's an awful lot of money! It's more than I'm spending on *all* our advertising!" My palms were sweating. I stood up to straighten the seams on my new red dress and paced once around my chair before sitting back down.

Steve Solomon, a dark-suited, serious man with a thoughtful face, explained, "The best way to get your company known is to publish some sort of survey or report on your marketplace. Something with a lot of numbers—the media love numbers. Maybe compare this year's prices to last year's."

"I guess that makes sense," I said, without a clue as to how I was going to get $750. "Could we call it something important, like the *New York City Apartment Price Report*?"

"Maybe," he replied diplomatically, jotting a few words down in his notebook. "Or how about calling it *The Corcoran Group Report*, or, even better, *The Corcoran Report*?"

"*The Corcoran Report*?" I paused and considered the sound of that. "But it doesn't mean anything," I said. "No one knows who or what Corcoran is."

"No," he answered, "but if you do the report, everyone soon will!"

Summer. Undercliff Avenue.

My hands were covered with chalk as I finished my master-piece and announced, "This is the largest sidewalk snail game in the history of the world!" The snail wriggled up and down the sidewalk, over the curb, and onto Undercliff Avenue. It stretched from Mrs. Rinebold's house, past Mrs. Gibbons's, and all the way up our front steps.

Square after square of symbols and shapes showed the neighborhood kids exactly what to do as they hopped onto each space: first with two feet, then one right foot, and the next commanding a left foot in reverse. Next came one of my tricky spirals I called "spinners," followed by a dozen other variations on and on to the end.

All the kids began lining up for their turn to hop, clap, jump, and spin their way around to the finish line.

As usual, Mean Michael Mertz was already standing at the head of the line. He darted through the first ten squares, pretending to almost trip on the reverse double spin, then bolted through the last forty spaces, making my snail look easy.

Fatty Patty stepped up next, and I just knew he was going to hurt himself. There was no way his chubby legs could possibly do a double spinner.

"Wait a minute, Patty!" I said, grabbing my pink chalk and walking over to the square. "I gotta fix one thing." I erased the spinner with the sole of my sneaker, drew two new easy feet in the same square, and stood up. "Okay, go ahead, Patty."

"*No way!*" Michael Mertz protested loudly. "You can't do that! You can't just go and change it like that!"

"Oh yes she can," Ellen said, defending me.

"No way, no how!" Michael repeated. "*You can't do that!*"

All the kids began shouting. It was Timmy Tom who broke the impasse when he peeped, "Why don't we ask Mrs. Corcoran, because *she's the mother.*"

I ran up the steps and into the kitchen. Mom was at her ironing board.

"Mom!" I blurted, trying to catch my breath. "Michael Mertz says I can't change one of the squares in my snail game. . . . Can I?"

"It's your game, Barbara Ann," she said, rendering her decision without lifting her eyes off Dad's white shirt. "Make up your own rules."

I bounded down the stairs, shouting Mom's verdict: "My mother says it's my game and I can make up my own rules!"

I stepped off the curb and stared Michael in the face. "And my rules are: It's *Patty's* turn!"

Fatty Patty finished the game on two solid feet, and I promised myself that tomorrow I'd make my snail even bigger! I'd start all the way up at the library, come down past the church, and wind it right back up Oxen Hill clear out of Edgewater!

July 1981. The Corcoran Group.

I slid a piece of our new Corcoran Group stationery into my Selectric typewriter. I stared at the blank page. I knew I had too few numbers to work with, but it was my game, and I was going to make up the rules.

The only information I had gathered for *The Corcoran Report* was a list of our apartment sales over the past six months, exactly eleven in total. So, I added up all the sale prices and divided by eleven. I checked it twice and the answer was $254,232. I rounded the figure up to an even $255,000 and typed in the words "AVERAGE NYC APARTMENT PRICE" next to it.

"There!" I said, surprising myself. "That was actually pretty easy and the average price seems about right to me."

I was feeling pretty smart and started thinking that a price *per room* might also be useful! So, I sat back and pictured all the apartments I had shown over the past few months and how many rooms each one had. I was writing fast. The algebra I had repeated twice in summer school was actually coming in handy.

So, let's see, I pondered, as I riffled through the stack of listing forms. *It looks like there are a lot more one-bedrooms than two-bedrooms, and a few more two-bedrooms than three-bedrooms. And since one-bedroom apartments have three or three and a half rooms, and two-bedrooms have four or four and a half rooms, and three-bedrooms have either five, six, or seven rooms, then*, I thought as I massaged my exploding head, *the average apartment in Manhattan must have about four and a quarter rooms!* "Yep, that's it," I decidedly said aloud, and began to type.

THE CORCORAN REPORT
1981 MID-YEAR STUDY

"An in-depth 6-month Survey and Analysis
of Conditions and Trends in the New York
City Luxury Apartment Marketplace."

AVERAGE APARTMENT PRICE: $255,000*

AVERAGE ROOM PRICE: $57,000*

*rounded up to the nearest thousand dol-
lars

For press inquiries contact:
Barbara Corcoran,
President, The Corcoran Group
212-355-3550

I yanked *The Corcoran Report* from the typewriter, made
sixty Xerox copies, and mailed one to every reporter who had
written an article in that Tuesday's *New York Times*. I even included the sportswriters, figuring that one of them might know
somebody rich, like Joe Namath, who might be looking to buy
a big apartment.

Sunday, August 30, 1981. New York Times.

I stared at the *New York Times* headline in disbelief:

STUDY SHOWS CO-OP PRICES NEARLY QUINTUPLED

The story read: "According to Barbara Corcoran, president of The Corcoran Group real estate company, the average price of apartments in New York City . . . has reached an all-time high of $255,000. . . ."

I read the line again more slowly and then once more out loud. I put the paper back down on my desk and thought, *I must be in the middle of some kind of Catholic miracle!*

I took out the scissors from my drawer and carefully cut out the words "According to Barbara Corcoran, president of The Corcoran Group real estate company." I coated the paper with some Cutex nail hardener, blew it dry, and taped it on my phone.

Two weeks after the release of our first *Corcoran Report*, I overheard one of my salespeople pitching for a listing on the phone. "I'm calling from The Corcoran Group," he said to the potential seller. "Let me spell it for you. It's *C-O-R-C*—oh, you've *heard* of us?!"

The *New York Times* story put me square in the middle of the Manhattan real estate game, playing it by my own rules.

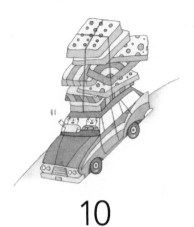

10

There's Always Room
for One More

1981. New York City.

Esther walked into my office and closed the glass door behind her. She was now hiring and training all of our salespeople, helping manage the office, and keeping our finances in check. In short, she was doing everything I had no time to do, making it possible for me to continue bringing in new business.

"Well?" I asked as she sat down after her latest round of interviews. "How were they? Any good ones?"

"I'd say that out of the bunch, the last two candidates were fairly good," Esther replied, tilting her head slightly to the left.

"But, Barbara . . ." By now I knew that any time Esther's head tilted to the left and she said, "But, Barbara," her left brain was going into overdrive. She went on, "Now that we have every desk filled and every salesperson productive and not an inch of space for a new desk anywhere, *why*, might I ask, are we interviewing more salespeople?"

Spring. Edgewater. The front steps.

Mom came out the screen door and leaned her broom against the house. "*Kids!*" she shouted, her belly protruding beneath her blue housedress. "Your dad will be coming down the hill any minute now with a *big* surprise!" We ran from the side yard to the front steps, each of us reaching our own conclusions about what the surprise might be. Mom stood on the top step with baby Mary Jean balanced on her hip, and we all sat below her and waited.

We heard Dad's green Rambler before we saw it. It clanked and growled like an old tanker. The used-car salesman had told Dad the Rambler "operates great in low gear!" So Dad had kept the engine in low gear for the first year he'd owned it.

"Here he comes!" Mom shouted, pointing left up the hill. We watched as Dad made the turn off Edgewater Place with Uncle Bobby in the passenger seat beside him. They were honking and waving from beneath what looked like a mountain of six-foot boxes atop the car's roof. Piled at least five high, they were bouncing and flapping as Dad's Rambler came down the hill.

"Those suckers are moving!" Eddie yelled, as Dad waved excitedly and we all waved back. The box tower leaned precariously to the left when Dad swerved to the right, and the Rambler screeched to a halt in front of our house.

"*Avalanche!*" Eddie yelled as ten twin mattresses thump-thump-thumped down the windshield and flipped onto the hood like dominoes. Uncle Bobby and Dad were still smiling and waving like beauty pageant winners on a wrecked float, their front doors webbed shut in clothesline.

Mom handed Mary Jean off to Denise and bounded down the steps two at a time. She arched her back and planted her hands squarely on her hips. "*Eddie!* You have *no* common sense. *None!* Why didn't you tie the rope in *both* directions? I'm telling you, Eddie, you're *just* like your father!"

"Sweetheart." Dad charmed her with a smile as he leaned through the clotheslined window. "Couldn't you get a knife or something and help get us out of here?"

While Mom ran up for the knife, swearing she'd use it on Dad, we all stampeded down to get a better look at our new mattresses. Some of them had little red stripes, some had blue ones, and a few had small green polka dots. In a mad frenzy, we each staked a claim on our favorite mattress.

After Mom cut through what seemed like a mile of clothesline, Dad and Uncle Bobby were freed from the Rambler and began taking the mattresses two at a time into our house.

Mom could always figure out a way to squeeze one more child into the boys' or girls' room. When Dad told Mom that the Holy Angel's Academy for Girls was closing, she had immediately sent him to get ten of its best twin-size mattresses while she spent the morning mentally rearranging our beds along each wall like railroad cars. Using her broom as a measuring stick to stake out each bed's space, Mom had calculated how to fit four twin beds into each room. As Dad and Uncle Bobby hoisted the mattresses into the house, she pointed out exactly where to put them.

"Girls' room!" she commanded. "Against the right wall. Boys' room"—she pointed—"to the left of the closet." Dad and Uncle Bobby huffed and puffed and followed Mom's instructions until four twin-size beds were neatly arranged in each room. "Now, put the crib in the living room between the wall and the sofa," she finished, "and take the two extra mattresses to the basement. We might end up needing them one day."

Esther sat with her hands neatly folded on her lap and her ankles crossed beneath her chair, primly waiting for my answer.

"The reason we're interviewing salespeople, my dear Esther, is because I've figured out a way to add more desks in our current space," I said smugly. "Probably *30 percent* more! I'll show you how it works."

I held up a manila folder on which I had drawn fourteen rectangles labeled "Desk," along with fourteen small circles labeled "Chair." "Here's a picture of what we have now," I said. "Seven desks on the left side and seven on the right, all facing in the same direction, separated by the aisle in the middle."

Then, allowing the folder to drop open like a hatch door, I revealed my drawing on the other side. "*Voilà!*" I said. "And here's our same office with a total of *twenty* desks. Ten on the left, ten on the right, and the same aisle down the middle."

I pointed to my sketch and explained, "The key, you see, is the space *between* the desks. If we place the desks front to front, facing each other, we eliminate every third passageway behind the chairs, and it gives us three more desks on each side."

Esther studied the "after" drawing with suspicion and counted the rectangles and circles once more. "But will we still have the same eighteen inches for each chair to move back and forth?" she asked. I assured her we would, as we went out to measure the sales area.

I grabbed the office broom and turned it horizontally to measure the depth of a single desk including its chair. Then I clasped both hands on the broomstick to mark the measurement, and, turning the length of the broom back and forth, back and forth, I measured and counted off the imaginary desks as

I went. The salespeople looked on, some smiling and others bewildered.

". . . eighteen, nineteen, twenty," I finished, and turned to Esther and said, "See? They'll fit. So let's hire those new people before someone else does!"

11

Go Play Outside

Winter 1982. New York City.

The New York real estate market was exploding and apartment prices were ballooning by the week. A new phenomenon called "overbidding" had just begun, adding another layer of stress on top of the already stressed-out sales environment. It seemed everyone in New York was making money—and had decided all at once to spend it on real estate. Everyone wanted New York, and my salespeople were totally exhausted.

I jumped into a cab on the way to my next afternoon showing, my thoughts bouncing between how I would get my next customer to make a high-enough bid on the one hand and how I'd get my salespeople to take a needed break on the other. At our Monday sales meeting, I had once again suggested that everyone plan some vacation time, but from the glazed expression on everyone's faces, I figured it wasn't likely to happen.

As my cab turned the corner onto Riverside Drive, I decided I'd better plan a vacation for them.

Winter. The side yard.

"*Snow day!*" Mom shouted from the living room.

Nothing could compare to the mornings we'd wake up and hear Mom's rare pronouncement of those most spectacular words. "Snow day" meant "no school."

We popped out of our beds, jumped into our playclothes, and headed for the front radiator, where Mom had already set up her snow day station. Our gloves were toasting on top of the radiator and our rubber boots warming below. Mom had lined up old cardboard boxes by the front door, along with her biggest cookie pans, a trash can lid, and anything else she could dig out of the basement or kitchen that could serve as a sled. We put on our boots, gloves, and mittens, and grabbed a makeshift sled. Mom gave us the once-over before pushing us out the door with her usual "Go play outside!"

Minutes before frostbite set in, we'd rush back in to the radiator's warmth, where Mom, like a pit crew in a car race, got us in and back out in thirty seconds flat. She yanked off our wet gloves and tossed them on top of the radiator to dry, giving each of us a pair of dry socks to put on our hands. She pulled off our boots, replaced our wet socks with dry ones, and sent us back outside. By day's end, the sock drawer was empty.

As traffic couldn't make it up or down River Road, Dad had the day off, too. Mom handed him Mary Jean and said, "Eddie, take a dishpan and fill it with snow for Tommy. He's feverish today, and I don't want him outside. I'll help him make snowballs in the bathtub."

After taking Tommy a dishpan of snow, Dad packed a snow-drift against the retaining wall that separated our front yard from the sidewalk. Then he dragged his two-story wooden ladder up to the very end of our backyard, the part that merged into the cliff behind our house.

"Hey, kids!" Dad yelled down, holding the ladder in place against the hill. "Hop on!"

We all raced to the top of the hill. "I call front!" Marty shouted, getting there first and taking the lead rung. The rest of us climbed on behind, locking our heels under the wooden rungs.

"Oh, no, you don't!" Eddie declared, pushing Marty off the ladder into the snow. "I'm the oldest, so I get the front."

Marty sprang up in a flash and reached back toward Eddie with a cocked fist. "Cut it out, boys!" Dad commanded. "Marty, either get on the ladder and have some fun, or we're leaving without you." Marty pouted into place on a middle rung.

"Ready?" Dad hollered, as we all stared downhill and clenched the side rails with our hands.

"Yes!" we yelled back in unison. Dad jostled the ladder side to side as though he were losing control.

"Are you *sure* you're ready?" he taunted.

"Yes. Oh, yes!" we pleaded back, overwhelmed with anticipation.

"Then let's get going!" And with a quick shove, Dad jumped on the back of the ladder and sent it lunging forward, zero to sixty in less than a second!

We all screamed as we zipped through the side yard, hurtling down toward Undercliff Avenue. We were picking up speed as we sailed toward the six-foot cinder-block retaining wall at the bottom. The front riders shrieked as their half of the ladder went airborne and momentarily waited for the back half to catch up.

Then, all at once, we shot off the ledge, sailed over the sidewalk, and thumped down squarely in the middle of the street, just behind a lone passing car that was sliding its way down Undercliff Avenue. We lay in the street, a jumbled pile of kids laughing until our sides and faces hurt.

Eddie offered Marty his hand and pulled him up. "Okay, Marty, you go first this time," he said. Eddie and Marty helped Dad lug the ladder back up the hill.

Mom was changing the sheets in the girls' room when she

spotted us flying past the side window. It was our third trip on Dad's death-defying ladder, and John caught a quick glimpse of Mom from the front rung. "It's Mom!" he gasped and pointed, as we plummeted toward the wall.

By the time we hit the street, Mom had barreled through the house, was down the steps, and had her face within two inches of Dad's. I noticed her blue slippers were soaked, and from what I could see, she looked cold and she sure looked angry. "*Eddie!*" she screamed. "*Eddie, you have no common sense, absolutely none!* Get the kids off the ladder NOW before you kill them," she shouted, seething, "or I swear, Eddie, I'll kill you!"

We cupped our socked hands over our mouths to choke back our laughter, until Dad leaked out his Cheshire cat smile. When we all exploded into a fit of laughter, even Mom began to laugh, and we knew for sure we had the best family in town.

1982. Snow day. Whaley Lake.

"*Ice-skating?!*" Esther repeated. "But I don't know *how* to skate!"

"That's just it," I told her as we sat in my office planning some fun. "*Nobody* does. But everybody will learn when they get there!"

I had just bought my first house for $75,000, a nine-room fixer-upper on Whaley Lake in Dutchess County. The house had six bedrooms, six bathrooms, two cabanas, two boathouses, and absolutely no land. My purchase was the classic example of buying the biggest house on the worst block. Twelve years later, I would sell it for . . . yep, $75,000.

"I have the whole weekend figured out, Esther," I continued, explaining my plans for our first company retreat. "I bought twenty pairs of ice skates for everyone, all in different sizes: white ones for the ladies and some black ones for the men. I also bought four sleds, eight sleeping bags for those who won't get beds, and twenty pairs of cheap wool mittens."

"*Cheap?*" Esther interrupted. "Nothing about this sounds cheap to me."

I dismissed Esther's look of concern with a quick wave of my hand and continued, "And I've talked my brother Tee into catering the whole weekend!"

"Tee? But isn't that brother a cabdriver?" she asked with growing concern.

"Yeah, but he got his weekend shift covered and he's bringing Judy Somebody, one of the other cabdrivers, and he says she's a really good cook."

Esther tilted her head.

"It'll all work out just fine," I went on. "And I got a great deal on a school bus to take everybody up on Friday night. We'll leave here around seven, and when we get there, the table will already be elegantly set, the flowers arranged, a fire burning, and a luscious meal will await us." I waited to see if Esther could picture it. "And after a great night's sleep, we'll all get up, eat a big breakfast, and have all day Saturday for ice-skating—and all day Sunday, too! We'll leave on Sunday around six and be back to the city no later than eight, eight thirty the latest."

Esther looked pale.

We opened our eyes Saturday morning to a crisp, icy-cold day. The night before had been just perfect. The bus showed up on time, the dinner was truly gourmet, and while we ate and drank, we talked about what our office needed, what we all wanted, and what we all dreamed about doing together. We came up with a flurry of new ideas, so I grabbed a piece of junk mail and jotted them down. I starred someone's idea to produce a *Corcoran Report* strictly on new condominium prices. I liked it because we had never sold a condominium and I wanted to get into that market. Then, like kids at a giant slumber party, we climbed into our beds and sleeping bags and fell asleep.

By nine A.M. on Saturday, we had finished breakfast and were all sitting on the boathouse ledge, juggling sizes and putting on our skates. Despite her inhibitions, Esther laced up first and desperately clung to the boathouse wall.

"You look like a natural over there, Esther," I joked, chinning in her direction. "Now, hurry up, everybody, we don't want to keep Dorothy Hamill waiting!"

Although this would be my first skate on Whaley Lake, it sure looked like the kind of lake you'd want to skate on. It was one mile long, a half mile wide, and frozen over as far as I could see.

Ron Rossi, our leading salesperson, glided out onto the ice. He was resplendent in a one-piece Bogner snowsuit with matching chartreuse gloves. His ensemble's finishing touch was a long magenta and yellow Hermès scarf, which floated behind him as he pushed off the boathouse wall. In a previous life, Ron had been a world champion ballroom dancer, and from the looks of his first spin, we suspected he had been on the ice before.

"Follow Ron!" I gushed, and like ducklings doing their first waddle, we all got behind him as he demonstrated a large figure eight. After a few hundred falls, Ron had us looping large figure eights back and forth, back and forth, farther and farther out onto the ice. Esther stayed behind, practicing her glide close to shore.

We were almost to the middle of the lake when I noticed we had attracted an audience on the shore. Squinting my eyes against the sun, I recognized the man in front of the old Gloyde's Motel as Old Man Gloyde himself. He was waving to us, and I waved back with enthusiasm. He shouted, "That's *nice*, that's *nice*!"

"*Thanks!*" I acknowledged in the loudest voice I could muster. "*Watch this!*" And with a quick tap of my right toe, I turned my left foot and went into my best amateur version of a twirl. I made a point of holding my hands straight out with pinkies up, just like Ron had taught us.

Mr. Gloyde seemed to like my twirl, because he waved even more vigorously, yelling again, "That's *nice*, that's *nice*!"

I was thinking about attempting a pretty pirouette, when I noticed Esther standing up on the boathouse ledge. She was waving just like Mr. Gloyde. When I heard the ice creak and begin to moan, it hit me. "Nice" wasn't "nice"—it was "ice." "Thin *ice*! Thin *ice*!" And we were skating on it!

"Let's get the *hell* out of here!" I screamed, and the entire Corcoran Group shrieked in unison as the ice under our skates began to crack. Our panicked feet raced toward the shore, every man for himself, as the splitting ice chased behind us. What must have been only two minutes at the most felt like a ten-mile run.

We all groped at Esther's legs as we clambered up onto the boathouse floor. We were huffing and puffing from our near-death experience. "You okay? You okay? You okay?" we chorused, as we scanned each other's faces. I looked around at my nineteen exhausted speed skaters, pulled off my hat, and started to laugh. With that, the whole boathouse rocked with laughter and I knew we had just become the best team in town.

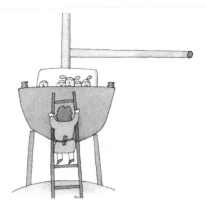

12

When the Clubhouse Is Quiet, They're Probably Not Making Spaghetti

Summer. Mrs. Harrison's backyard.

We found Charlie's boat wedged inside the big chicken shed in Mrs. Harrison's backyard. The Harrisons lived three doors up in a house almost identical to ours. But rather than having three families on three floors, Mrs. Harrison had only three kids and rented the rest of her rooms to eight old men.

The great thing about the chicken shed was its roof. It was the only place from which we could reach Old Maid Stella's cherry tree. Stella's tree hung high over her fence, leaving count-less juicy cherries dangling just out of reach above our heads in the Harrison yard. But we could climb onto the shed's roof, shimmy over to the edge, and pick a handful of fruit. Stella's third-floor window looked onto the roof and she was always peeking out trying to catch us stealing her cherries.

"*Aaaaaah!*" Skinny Timmy Tom Harrison screamed one hot afternoon. "It's Stella the Cherry Witch!" We all looked up to see Stella's baggy, saggy eyes glaring at us from behind her chenille curtains. "She's got her broom! Run for your lives!" Stella opened the window and threw her broom at us like a javelin, and we took off across the tin roof. "Follow me!" Timmy Tom squawked, his skinny legs running ahead of him across the roof. Like a superhero, he leapt into the air, landing midway up the cliff that climbed dramatically behind the Harrison house.

"*Psst!* In here!" He beckoned us, opening the tiny window in the old shed behind their house. I jumped off the roof with Kathy Harrison, Janet Cleary, Michael Mertz, and my brother Tee following. We scurried through the window and dropped into the cool, shadowy corner of the Harrisons' old shed.

We were huffing and puffing, our little hearts racing. "Oh my gosh," I gulped, leaning against the inside wall. "Did you see her eyes? They were glowing as red as her cherries!" A few beams of light streaked through the windows, splashing light over the contents of the shed. "What's *that*?" I gasped at the giant hulking structure looming above us, twice as tall as any of us.

"That's Charlie's boat," Timmy Tom explained. "He's been

building it in here with his own hands since I was three. He said he's gonna sail away on that boat."

"It's beautiful!" Janet Cleary gushed as she caressed the bottom of the boat, feeling its smooth, shiny wood. The boat ran from one end of the shed to the other.

"Hey, let's get in," I said, already climbing the ladder.

"Be careful!" Michael Mertz warned. "It might be dangerous."

"Are you a *scaredy cat*, Michael Mertz?" I taunted.

"I'm not scared of nothing," he said, following me up.

One by one we climbed up the ladder onto the deck of Charlie's boat and then stepped down below into its cabin. Though unfinished, the boat was already outfitted with tin kitchenware and two blue blankets. "This will be our new clubhouse!" I declared. It was clearly the greatest clubhouse in the world. "Who wants to join?" Everyone raised their hands. "It's our *secret* clubhouse," I said. "Only us and no one else can know. Understand?" Everyone nodded their heads. "We'll have to seal the secret. Michael Mertz, you first."

"Whadda I gotta do, Barbara Ann?" he asked.

"Show us your heinie," I said. Without blinking, Michael Mertz dropped his pants, and as the light poured into the cabin of our new clubhouse, we all stared at Michael Mertz's little white eight-year-old behind.

After four more sets of cheeks were shown, I declared the first meeting of the Showing Heinies Club officially over.

"Tomorrow at noon," I whispered as we all climbed out of

the boat, "and don't tell anyone, *not anyone!*" I felt I might be doing something wrong and figured with a mom like Mom, I didn't want to get caught.

On the fifth day of our Showing Heinies Club, five pairs of white cheeks were shining like harvest moons when the shed door swung open.

"It's Charlie!" I whispered, as we all squatted down, paralyzed and exposed.

"Who's up there?" Charlie hollered. "I know somebody's in there." The boat sat quiet, five naked behinds momentarily frozen in time. Then the boat rocked in its wooden cradle as all of us scrambled to pull up our pants. "Who's in there?" Charlie demanded.

I grabbed a metal plate and fork and banged a few of Charlie's tin Coleman pots around, trying to make as much noise as possible to disguise the sounds of snapping buttons and zipping zippers. "We're making spaghetti, Charlie," I shouted. "Just making spaghetti."

One by one, five guilty faces popped over the edge of the boat and peered down at the old blond Swede. "It's just me," Timmy Tom peeped. "And me." "And me." "And me." "And me," the rest of the fanny five admitted.

"Making spaghetti, huh?" the old Swede said. "All right, but be careful in there. I'm going to sail away in that boat at the end of the summer."

On the eighth day of the Showing Heinies Club, we were right in the middle of Michael Mertz's turn when we heard my mom's voice outside the shed. "What are the kids doing in there, Charlie?" Mom asked. We all held our breath.

"Oh, they're fine, Mrs. Corcoran," he told her. "They're just making spaghetti."

"Nope, Charlie," she said. "When the clubhouse is quiet, they're *never* making spaghetti!" With that, she barged into our clubhouse, grabbed me and Kathy Harrison with one hand, told Michael to pull up his pants, and sent everybody home.

Summer 1983. Monday-morning meeting.
The Corcoran Group.

We were right in the middle of a long, hot summer in New York. City streets and tempers alike steamed in the high temperatures. Our salespeople were happy to be in our air-conditioned office between showings, and this Monday morning they were all at their desks for our regular sales meeting, sipping the iced lemonade I had substituted for coffee. I took a deep breath, bracing myself to do what I had carefully planned to do.

Everyone at The Corcoran Group knew the company listing policy, which I had established at our very first sales meeting. Our "share and share alike" policy required that salespeople post all new listings in our office files within one hour of getting the property. Our policy was understood and welcomed, as it set us apart from the other firms' "every man for himself"–type policies. Their salespeople pocketed listings for their special customers, keeping them secret from coworkers they viewed as competitors. In contrast, we shared all our listings. At least, that was the idea.

Elaine had joined our company two summers earlier and quickly became our single best lister. She was French and quiet, and spent most of her time outside our office. When she was in the office, her only activity was opening her middle drawer, exchanging papers from her brown leather briefcase, and scurrying out, her eyes darting from side to side.

Over the past month, Elaine's listing numbers had dwindled, and in the past week, she had not added a single new listing to the company files. Paranoia was creeping into our happy home, and the warm hello I had extended to Elaine that morning had been returned with a quick dart of her blue-eye-linered eyes. I had had enough.

"Good morning, everyone!" I began as usual.

"Good morning, Barbara," everyone replied.

"Today I'd like to start our meeting by reviewing our listing policy," I said. "One of the big differences between our firm and the others is that we share and share alike. We work hard and we play fair. I'd like to restate our policy that all new listings must be posted for everyone within one hour of getting the property. I want to remind everyone again that 'pocket listings' won't be tolerated. Does anyone have any new listings they want to put in the listing card files today?"

Everyone shook their heads no, including Elaine.

"How about you, Elaine?" I asked as I walked over to her desk. "Would you have any listings to add to our company file today?"

"*Non*," she replied.

"Okay," I said. "Then would you mind opening up your second drawer?"

"Nothing ees in dere," she protested. "Juste old papers."

"You'll have to excuse me, Elaine," I said, opening her drawer and removing the rubber-banded pile of papers, chock-full of listing information. I pulled out the top paper from the rest and read it aloud to the room. "Could anyone tell me if we have apartment 4B at 60 Sutton Place South listed for $340,000?" Everyone shook their heads a tense, slow no. "It sounds nice," I continued. "It's a two-bedroom, two-bath with a terrace!

"How about apartment 12D at 1065 Park?" Again they signaled no. I quickly flipped through the thirty or so sheets, each with a different address. Then I turned to Elaine and asked, "Elaine, is there any reason you haven't put these listings in our company files?"

Her lips quietly mouthed, "*Non.*"

"Pack your things," I said. "And if you don't mind, I'll keep these pocket listings."

We all watched as Elaine quickly shoved her desk items into her brown briefcase and huffed out the office door.

The moment the door closed, the whole office erupted in cross-chatter, a mix of astonishment and relief. I took the pile of Elaine's papers and dealt them out like a blackjack dealer.

I had caught Elaine with her pants down and in the process charted a moral course for our company's future.

13

If You Want to Be a Cheerleader, You Better Know the Cheers

September 12, 1985

Dear Mr. Trump,
I thought you might like to see this before I send it to the press.

Best regards,

Barbara Corcoran
President
The Corcoran Group

I clipped my note to The Corcoran Group's new *Top 10 Condominium Report* and sealed the envelope. "Trump Tower," I said, handing it to the messenger, "the penthouse."

Donald Trump built a billion-dollar real estate empire with shameless self-promotion and sheer chutzpah. He was the best known businessman in the city and his name was synonymous with everything New Yorkers both loved and hated about New York. Mr. Trump's latest enterprise, Trump Tower, was a sixty-eight-story black glass condominium next door to Tiffany's, at 57th Street and Fifth Avenue. He was promoting his new building as "the most expensive address in the world." Only in New York could "most expensive" be a badge of honor, and the Donald wore it with pride. I wanted The Corcoran Group name to scream New York real estate as loudly as Mr. Trump's did, and I had a plan.

My *Top 10 Condominium Report* didn't list Trump's trophy property in first place, second, or even third. The sales data I had collected relegated his building to fourth position behind Museum Tower, Olympic Tower, and the Galleria, Trump's main rivals in town.

I'd never met Mr. Trump, but I knew my latest report would sizzle in his hands. Sure enough, within an hour, he called.

Cheerleading tryouts. High school.

I finished the Holy Rosary School in Edgewater as a charity D student. After my special reading class with Sister Stella Marie in second grade, school only got worse. After graduation from eighth grade, the Catholic kids with the good grades all went to the Catholic high schools, and everybody else was bused two towns over to the public school in Leonia.

I was shocked when an acceptance letter from St. Cecilia's Catholic High School arrived at the end of eighth grade. I thought it had to be a mistake, that they'd put the right slip in the wrong envelope. A chance at St. Cecilia's seemed like the light at the end of a long, dark school tunnel. I promised my parents and myself that at my new school I would do a lot better.

On my first day at St. Cecilia's, the homeroom teacher asked me to be our student council representative. He picked me because Corcoran started with *C*. I sat in the second seat, behind Maureen Beckman, who would have been selected because her name started with a *B*, but she had already left when the bell rang. He handed me a list of questions to poll and collect the opinions of the other homeroom kids. The survey gave me the opening I needed to befriend my new classmates.

I was well on the road to popularity at St. Cecilia's when I flunked algebra, history, and Latin, and just as Dad had warned, I soon was taking the bus up the hill for my sophomore year at the public high school in Leonia. I had blown my one chance to be somebody.

I looked up at the notice posted on the big bulletin board hanging outside the Leonia High School gym:

CHEERLEADER TRYOUTS
WEDNESDAY THRU FRIDAY
3 to 5 P.M.
IN THE GYM

It was obvious in my first two weeks at my new school that the popular girls were all from Leonia, not from Edgewater. And the *really* popular ones were the cheerleaders. They were pretty, they had nice clothes, and they were always surrounded by guys. They were everything I was not and wanted to be.

That's it! I said to myself, looking at the poster. *I'm taking the fast road to popularity!* I printed my name on the sign-up sheet in the 4:45 Thursday spot.

I pushed open the heavy metal door of the large gym and realized it didn't look any bigger than the gym at St. Cecilia's. A cafeteria table was set up at the far end below the basketball hoop, and I noted the backboard above it read "away." I thought it might be a bad sign.

Three women sat behind the table. I figured they were the judges. I recognized one as the gym teacher and guessed the other two women were probably teachers, too. Six cheerleaders were huddled in a sideline giggle, looking like burgundy-and-gold best friends. I clicked my way across the polished floor to center court. When the cheerleaders built a perfect pyramid, I panicked, wondering if I was expected to know how to build a pyramid, too.

"Name, please," the gym teacher asked.

"Hi, I'm Barbara." I waved. "And I have an appointment for a four forty-five tryout."

"Yes, Miss Corcoran," the woman said, checking her clipboard. "Please remove your shoes." I took off my loafers, set them next to me, and faced the panel of judges in my stocking feet. I wished I had brought my sneakers.

Everyone turned their attention to me, including the pyramid, which quickly toppled and formed a perfect line to watch.

"Okay, then," the gym teacher said.

"Okay, what?" I asked.

"Let's see your cheer."

"What cheer?"

"Whichever cheer you choose."

That's when I realized I wasn't prepared. Not only did I not

know a cheer; I hadn't ever even *seen* a Leonia cheer. I had to
think fast. I figured the name they probably liked best was Leonia. It was also the safest word for me to spell. So I spread my
legs in an official cheerleader-type stance, puffed out my chest,
shoved my fists into my hips, and began:

"Give me an *L*!" I shouted.

Silence.

"*L*!" I shouted back to myself, throwing my right arm and leg
out to the side.

"Give me an *E*!"

"*E*!" I answered. Not knowing what part to use, I swung my
arm and leg like a windmill in the other direction.

When I finally made it to the "And what does it spell?" part,
even I didn't answer.

I dropped my arms, smiled my best cheerleader-type smile,
raising my lower lip to cover my overbite, and felt the red blotches
begin to form on my chest.

"Thank you," the teacher said, as she drew a line on her
clipboard.

I felt like an absolute *idiot*! I wished the floor could have
swallowed me up! I gave a quick nod to the cheerleading squad
and finally moved my legs and walked out of the gym.

Sitting in the back of the late-afternoon bus, I tried to engrave
the faces of the six cheerleaders in my mind. I felt really bad

about hating them but knew I'd spend the next three years avoiding them between classes. The bus dropped me off at the top of Hilliard Avenue, and I found Mom outside on the Roanes' landing, hanging diapers out to dry. She pinned the corners two at a time and listened to my tale of woe.

". . . And if that wasn't bad enough, Mom," I explained, blinking back the moisture in my eyes, "I left my loafers in center court and had to go back and walk in front of *everyone* to get them!"

Mom clipped her last diaper to the line, gave me a wry smile, and said, "Well, Barbara Ann, next time you try out for cheerleading, you better know the cheers."

"Well, how obvious!" I snapped. "That's really, really helpful, Mom!" And with a quick look of indignation, I stomped into the house and ran up to the new girls' room, on the third floor. The four girls had moved into the third floor of our house when Aunt Ethel and Uncle Herbie moved out and retired to Toms River.

I reached under my mattress to where I had stashed my new box of filtered Parliaments and lit a cigarette.

1985. Trump Tower. Meeting the King.

I knew I wouldn't compromise my *Top 10 Condominium Report* by changing any facts. But I also knew Mr. Trump would be outraged by his lowly ranking, and I didn't want my report to alienate an industry figure as powerful as Donald Trump. So I had spent the weekend working the numbers every which way and had figured out a way to do both. Once I had found a solution, I practiced a routine on how to deliver it at least a dozen times. I stood in the elevator of Trump Tower with my heart racing but my confidence intact.

The elevator doors opened onto a reception area bigger than The Corcoran Group's entire office and backdropped with floor-to-ceiling views of Central Park. I stood in my new red suit atop all of New York.

A drop-dead gorgeous receptionist sat at the far end at a burled-wood desk. She was answering the phone. "Good morning, the Trump Organization," she said in a continuous loop. She was saying it with a lot more importance than I had ever been able to muster up for "Good morning, Giffuni Brothers." I made my way over to her desk and stood waiting to say hello. She looked to me like a beauty queen, the kind you see on TV.

"Hi," I finally interrupted, offering my hand across her desk. "I'm Barbara Corcoran and I have an appointment with Mr. Trump."

She didn't look up but lilted into an intercom, "*Bahr-bruh Cohr-krun* here to see Mr. Trump." Another beauty queen instantly appeared to escort me down a long wood-paneled hall. There yet another beauty queen asked that I follow her down another hall and passed me on to another woman who, unlike the others, looked like the kind of person who could get some work done.

"Hello," she said with authority. "I'm Louise Sunshine. We spoke on the phone. If you'll wait here, I'll see if he's ready." She cracked a set of gigantic doors, stepped inside, and closed the doors behind her.

I thought about my new *Top 10 Condominium Report*. As it was customary in New York to refer to apartments based on their sales price, my report ranked the ten top-selling condos from the highest to the lowest sale price. I had pulled the figures from the *Yale Robbins Condo Sales Report* and had also cross-checked each sale against the city's transfer files to make sure my numbers were absolutely correct.

A few moments later, the doors opened. "Mr. Trump will see you now," the woman announced, as she invited me into an office the size of an aircraft carrier.

Mr. Trump was seated behind a landing strip of a desk flanked by a panoramic view of Central Park. The woman gestured toward the two leather chairs positioned in front of his desk and announced, "Mr. Trump, this is Barbara Corcoran."

I walked over and extended my hand. When Mr. Trump took my hand, I filed it in my memory as the wimpiest handshake of all time. "I *really* appreciate your coming over," he said cordially, sizing me up and whisking his puffed blond helmet to the side. "Have a seat."

Before I reached the seat, he began, "I got your report and I don't agree with it. Your information is totally incorrect because there's sales data on Trump Tower you don't have access to."

As prepared as I'd thought I was, I was startled by his opening move and felt my palms getting sticky. "Oh, really," I said politely, "and just what information is that, Mr. Trump?"

He leaned forward into the intercom that sat on the left corner of his desk and barked, "Norma! Bring me those condominium numbers!" The giant doors opened and a June Cleaver look-alike floated in, plunked a thick folder on Mr. Trump's otherwise clean desk, and floated out. He puckered his lips, opened the file, and leaned confidently back in his chair. "If you'll take the time to look at these *recent* numbers," he emphasized, "it will be obvious to you that Trump Tower belongs at the top of your list!" He pushed the file in my direction, just out of reach.

I tried to move my chair closer to His Majesty's to get a peek at the numbers, but the chair wouldn't move. I stood up, took one giant step forward, opened the file, scanned the typed columns of sale prices, and recognized the information as the same data I had already used for my report. *So far, so good*, I thought, knowing I had regained my footing.

"Mr. Trump," I said, "I'm pleased to say that each of these transactions was already *included* in my calculation." I smiled at him. "But I sure do appreciate your sharing them with me, sir."

Mr. Trump pursed his lips and bellowed into his intercom.

"Marsha! Bring your calculator and come in here!" When the big doors parted again, an Ivana look-alike entered and strode across the floor in va-vooms to Mr. Trump's desk. Va-voom, va-voom, va-voom. She bent down, her cleavage eye level with Mr. Trump, and entered numbers as he rattled them off. When she came up with the same totals I already had, the ones that placed Trump Tower squarely in fourth place, Va-voom was immediately dismissed.

Mr. Trump was clearly becoming more frustrated and barked again into his intercom: "Joe! Get in here! And bring those Trump Tower deals we were just talking about this morning." Joe muscled in, a compact man in a too-tight suit. He reminded me of Rocky Rocciano, the drummer I'd dated from Garfield High. Joe handed a sheet of paper to Mr. Trump and muscled out. Mr. Trump nodded, passing the paper my way. "Have a look at *these* sales!" he said glibly.

I surveyed the sheet of twenty sale prices, each belonging to an apartment I hadn't seen before. The prices were much higher than the others, and Mr. Trump smirked when he saw the surprise register on my face. I shifted in my seat, trying to get my routine back on track. "Could I see the dates on each of these transactions, Mr. Trump?" I asked.

To my relief, he bragged, "They were all sold this weekend, Barbara! All twenty of them! I tell you, it's incredible, really incredible!"

"That really *is* incredible, Mr. Trump!" I agreed. "And if they had *closed* this weekend, I could have included those sales in my report."

Mr. Trump winced, and I noticed his hair looked like cotton candy backlit by the western sky. "Listen," he said, enunciating each word, "everyone knows that Trump Tower is the most expensive address in the world, and putting anything else in your report will be inaccurate."

The time had come for my grand finale, the moment to trump Mr. Trump.

"Mr. Trump," I began, "it's very important to me that I make you happy." I spoke slowly. "But I also need to publish a *truthful* report. Surely, there must be *something* you could think of that would make the report work for both of us."

I waited a few moments, and then, I made the move I had practiced a dozen times the night before. "Wait, wait just a minute!" I said, as if a lightbulb had just popped on in my head. I stood up and walked purposefully around to Mr. Trump's side of the desk, leaning my forearm on his shoulder. "Let's see," I said, pointing to the Trump sale prices in my report. I paused a moment for dramatic effect. "What if we were to compute the prices on a *cost per foot basis*, instead of the total sale price like everyone else does? I wonder what that would do?"

I circled the highest-priced sale at Trump Tower, which was $3,033,500, divided it by its 2,509 square feet, and spit out the answer faster than a calculator. "Why that's $1,209 a square foot!" I concluded, drawing a circle around apartment 62L with an arrow moving it straight to the top of my list. I quickly divided Trump's next two most expensive sales by their square footage, circled those answers, and moved them into second and third place.

"That's it! You've got it!" Trump enthused. "And I was just going to suggest it." The King of the Least for the Most was obviously pleased. "You know, Barbara, it puts Trump Tower exactly where it belongs—unmistakably the most expensive address in the world!"

"And it's also honest," I said. I walked back around to the front of his desk and offered my hand. "Thank you, Donald," I said. "You're a brilliant man and I really appreciate meeting you."

My new best friend stood up, gave me his limp handshake, and said, "You'll send me the revised report, won't you?"

"I'd be happy to."

"Today?"

"Sure," I said. "I'll send it over by messenger this afternoon."

As the brass-paneled elevator door shut, I caught the image of myself in my new red power suit. I put my hands on my hips, looked straight into my eyes, and told my own reflection to:

"Give me a Y! . . . Y!" I answered.

"Give me an E! . . . E!" I answered.

"Give me an S! . . . S!" I answered.

"What does it spell?"

"YES!" I cheered, thrusting my fist into the air.

This time, I knew I had made the team.

Two days after the *Top 10 Condominium Report* was released to the press, Esther walked into my office holding a copy of the *Wall Street Journal*. I could read the full-page ad from where I sat:

TRUMP TOWER
TOPS THE LIST
AS THE MOST
EXPENSIVE ADDRESS
IN THE WORLD! *

The asterisk referenced a bolded footnote at the bottom of the page. It had the words I'd most hoped to see: **Source: *The Corcoran Report***.

The phone rang and I recognized Donald Trump's voice on the other end. "Hello, Barbara. Have you seen this morning's paper?"

"Yes, I have. I'm looking at it now."

"Well, how do you like it?" he asked with Trump-size confidence.

"I like it a lot," I said, "but I wish you could have made our name a little bigger."

The following Monday, I opened the *New York Times* to yet another full-page ad.

ACCORDING TO
THE CORCORAN REPORT,
TRUMP TOWER
IS THE MOST EXPENSIVE
ADDRESS IN THE WORLD!

With equal billing in Trump's advertisement, The Corcoran Group became recognized as a major player in the New York real estate game.

14

Go Stand Next to Nana and See How Big You Are!

Fall 1985. Citibank Center.

"With a sales staff of over fifty people and offices in Midtown and the Upper West Side . . ."

The moderator's voice boomed through the auditorium of Citibank's corporate headquarters. I was being introduced to an audience of 800 people, about 750 more than I'd ever addressed.

". . . And Ms. Corcoran publishes *The Corcoran Report*, today considered the bible of the New York real estate market. . . ."

Citibank's invitation to speak at their company's first Seminar for Home Buyers had caught me by surprise. When the man from the bank's events department called, he enthusiastically explained that my recent comments on home buying in the *Wall Street Journal* made me an ideal speaker for their new seminar. And, he promised, the featured speakers would be well promoted weeks before the event. I figured that kind of free advertising would be great for my business.

"I have no doubt Ms. Corcoran's tips on home buying will help you. . . ."

It was my first public speech and I had worked on it for three weeks, editing every word and rehearsing its delivery over and over again. With *The Quick and Easy Way to Effective Speaking* as my guide, I had typed the first line of each of my paragraphs in caps on separate index cards. I was ready!

". . . So please join me in welcoming the president of The Corcoran Group, Barbara Corcoran!"

The audience broke into applause. I stood up, raised my chin to create just the right look of confidence, and made my way behind the two other chairs to center stage. *You are a PROfessional speaker!* a happy little voice in my head whispered. *You're a natural, a real natural!* I stepped behind the podium and gracefully placed my left hand on the edge. I took one serious look down at my notes, looked up at the audience, flashed my best smile, and with a quick wave of my right hand chirped, "Hello there!"

I had decided to open Cosby-style, with a joke. "Did you

hear the one about the banker who was a *great lover*?" I began. I leaned into the podium, waiting for the audience's reply. Sixteen hundred eyes stared back at me, but not one person offered a response. The little voice inside my head encouraged, *Go on, go on, you're doing fine!* But something in my heart made me start to wonder.

When I realized that the audience was waiting for the punch line, I decided I'd better give them the answer. *Oh my God*, my mind shrieked. *What is the punch line?* I quickly looked down at index card number one. It read, "Did you hear the one about the banker who's a great lover?" That was all. I shuffled the card to the back of my deck and sneaked a peek at card number two. And it read, "What's your budget?" That was all it said.

I began to panic and the little voice inside my head began to scream, *Why didn't you write the answer, stupid? Just think! Say something! Say* anything! No matter how hard I tried, I just couldn't remember the punch line. I smoothed down the front of my new red suit, took a big breath, and decided to move on.

When I looked back down at my "What's your budget?" card, the words had turned blurry. But I knew the rest of this point anyway and started to speak, but nothing came out. I tried to cough but couldn't. I tried again to speak, make a sound, any sound, but I couldn't. I realized that my voice wasn't going to come out, not tonight, not any night, not ever again.

I glanced over at the moderator, and he looked as scared as I felt. So I turned to the audience and opened my mouth as wide as I could. Pointing to the mute hole, I slowly shook my head no. I turned and took what seemed to be a very long walk back to my seat.

The moderator jumped up and rushed to the microphone. "Okay . . ." he said, looking bewildered. "Thank you, Barbara! And we'll be hearing more from her later. Next, I'd like to introduce Citibank's leading mortgage specialist. . . ."

I spent the rest of the event frozen in my chair, numbly staring at the Citibank logo on the wall.

I was still burning from public humiliation as I got home and sank into a hot bath. The night's calamitous scene played again and again in my mind; with each rerun I grew smaller and smaller.

Winter. The kitchen table.

We had been sent home that Friday afternoon with our midyear report cards and the sisters' usual instructions to bring them back Monday morning along with our parents' signatures. We all anxiously waited at the kitchen table as Dad looked over and signed our cards one by one.

"That's excellent work, Ellen." He beamed, looking down her column of As and signing "Rock Hudson" at the bottom. Everyone laughed and Ellen leaned over his shoulder to have a better look. "And you did a nice job there, Tommy, but let's turn that B in gym into an A next time." Tommy danced off through the living room with Eliot Ness's signature. Awaiting Mr. Corcoran's signatures had become a quarterly event for the Saint Joseph's sisters at the Holy Rosary School. They always looked forward to the Mondays we brought our signed report cards back.

"Eddie," Dad continued, shifting his voice into low gear, "four Fs are two too many! Another three months' garbage duty for you! Now for you, Barbara Ann," Dad said, as he took my report card in his hand and I took a quiet step back toward the refrigerator. "Well, at least you're consistent. Straight Ds from top to bottom!" All the kids laughed as Dad handed me the report card, signed by Pat Boone.

I ran to my room, jumped onto my bed, and buried my face in the pillow, feeling ashamed to be so stupid.

"Barbara," Mom said as she sat on the edge of my bed, "don't be so hard on yourself; straight Ds aren't that bad. And besides, Sister Joseph Marie always tells me you're the nicest girl in the whole class." I turned my head to look at my mother. "Now," she said, "get yourself up and go stand next to Nana and see how big you are."

Nana was almost four feet eight inches tall but picked up another two inches as she trotted around the house in her everyday pumps. She was standing next to the sofa and folding towels on the coffee table. Nana's big white pocketbook, the constant companion that scraped the ground as she walked, was looped around her left arm.

"Hi, Nana," I said. "Mom sent me to see how big I am." Nana smiled as she took off her shoes and turned her back against mine.

"Oh, look!" she exclaimed over her shoulder. "You're even bigger than last time!" I gave Nana a hug, she put on her shoes, and I ran out the screen door to go play with my friends.

The morning after my Citibank debacle, I picked up the New York University Continuing Education circular from my desk and called the phone number listed on the back. "I'd like to teach a course," I told the nice woman at the school.

"Oh, on what subject?" she asked sweetly.

"A course on what every real estate salesperson should know," I said, quickly adding, "and I'm more than qualified to teach. I've hired and trained more than fifty salespeople, I have great material, and I'm also an *excellent* speaker!"

"Well, then, why don't you submit a course outline and send it to the program office care of Mr. Neil Boffey," she suggested. "If he likes it, he'll pass it along to the program committee, who may approve it for the summer program."

I smiled and put down the phone.

June 1986. New York University.

My seven students appeared to be a contingent sent over from the United Nations. Just like the rest of New York, they were a smorgasbord of different nationalities and they were all serious about being there. Since most of the seats were empty, I decided there must have been a mix-up in the room number given to the students and delayed starting the class. I hoped that another dozen or so students would be arriving late to fill the desks.

"We'll begin class in about five minutes," I announced, "to give the other students a chance to arrive. But while we wait, why don't we go around the room and introduce ourselves to one another? Please speak up, give us your name first, and then, if you'd like, tell me what you hope to get out of the class over the next ten weeks." I listened and smiled as the students introduced themselves.

"Let me also introduce myself to you. I'm Barbara Corcoran, president of The Corcoran Group." I took a quick look down at my notes and said, "Since it looks tonight as though we're only going to be seven, let's begin."

No sooner had I said "seven" than the door banged open and a Chinese woman hurried in. She walked directly to the center front desk and said to the man sitting there, "I want to sit there." The man looked confused and started to move.

"There's another seat in the front over here," I quickly interrupted. "And it also has a better view of the blackboard. As everyone just finished introducing themselves, why don't you take a seat and introduce yourself to the class?"

"Carrie Chiang," she blurted, and then hustled over to the desk on the other side of the room and plopped herself down. While I went over the classroom rules, she riffled through her papers and unpacked her bags.

"I was asked to announce that smoking and eating in the classroom are not permitted, but as six thirty is my dinner hour, you're welcome to bring food, as long as you leave the room as clean as you found it." The woman hiding her sandwich looked relieved. "You'll find the restrooms down the hall and we'll be taking a break in about an hour. Last, I'm pleased to announce that everyone will earn an A for taking this course simply because you came. Your outline is in front of you, so let's get started." The students seemed to like my A idea and smiled.

The best way to get over my Citibank debacle was to move on, and I knew I could do that only by practicing speaking in front of a large group. Although lecturing to eight students wasn't exactly what I'd had in mind, I looked at the class and figured some practice was better than no practice at all.

An hour later, I declared a class break and walked down the hall to the school cafeteria. I had made up my mind to cancel the remaining nine classes and would announce it right after the break. Giving up three hours every Monday night for ten weeks over the summer just wasn't going to be worth it.

As I reached for the wilted fruit salad, I was startled to hear my name. "Baa-bwa!" the Chinese woman called as she cut into the line and made her way toward me. "Baa-bwa, you know how long I been in business? You know how long?"

"No, I don't," I answered, picking up a bagel and cream cheese from the counter. "How long has it been?"

"T'ree months," she bragged.

"Three months?" I repeated.

"You know how much money I make in t'ree months?"

"No, I don't," I said, surprised that someone would offer so much information so quickly, especially in a crowded cafeteria line.

"*Two, hundred, dousand, dollars!*" she boasted, loud enough for the buzz in the line to come to a complete stop. "I sell only condos," she said. "I sell lots of condos!"

"Selling condos?" I replied. "How can you make that much money selling only condos?!" I took a closer look at her, trying to pick up anything that lacked credibility. But everything about her looked like the genuine article: her blunt-cut, neatly combed hair, her solid gold choker, her well-tailored sweater set with three buttons open and three buttons closed. Even her black mid-height heels, supporting two sturdy legs, looked as if they meant business. Miss Chiang started speaking in a rapid-fire Chinese-American dialect, gesturing frantically as she spoke.

"I sell *big* condos to big customer in Hong Kong!" she rattled, opening up her leather file and pulling out a manila folder.

"He's a *big* customer; he send me his cousin and his cousin buy small condo. Dis lady have sister-in-law in Taiwan and she buy *two* condos! She send me sister's *cousin* in Hong Kong, but she no good. But she send me cousin from Taiwan and she buy *more* condo!"

I immediately switched gears from snoozing to schmoozing, realizing I had just stepped in front of the Hong Kong to Taiwan to New York express. "That's *really* incredible!" I said admiringly. "You're *just amazing!*" I gave Miss Chiang my very best smile and decided the ten weeks might be worth it after all!

By the time the NYU semester ended, Carrie Chiang had arrived at our office along with her leather file, her twelve boxes of folders, and her first cousin working as her assistant.

When Carrie started in 1986, the condominium market accounted for less than 5 percent of the city's residential sales. By late 2002, New York's burgeoning condo market accounted for more than 35 percent of city sales. And Carrie Chiang, New York's number one undisputed condo queen, had sold more condos than anyone else.

By teaching classes at NYU over the next five years, I succeeded in becoming an excellent public speaker, and the course proved to be my most fertile ground for recruiting top-notch salespeople. Not a bad payoff for standing back up.

15

If You Want to Get Noticed,
Write Your Name on the Wall

Summer. Mrs. Cacciotti's.

"Barbara Ann!" my mother said sharply with her hands on the waist of her blue housedress. "Did *you* write your name on Mrs. Cacciotti's wall?"

"Why, Mom?" I answered, trying to buy a little time.

"Don't you 'why' me, Barbara!" she commanded. "*Did* you?"

"I *think* so," I said with hesitation.

"Well, then, Barbara, if you *think* so, you better start *thinking* about coming with me!" Mom grabbed my wrist and yanked me out the screen door. From how fast we were walking, I was starting to get the feeling I might be in trouble.

Mrs. Cacciotti's house was four doors down, and with each step toward it, I was growing more fearful. Mrs. Cacciotti had called only minutes ago, so I knew Mom hadn't actually *seen* what I'd done.

For two whole weeks, Janet Cleary, Eugene Darby, and I had met on the strip of grass across the street from Mrs. Cacciotti's house and watched the three men build a long retaining wall in front of her house. As they laid the cement blocks one by one, they didn't talk much, but from the few words they said, we knew they weren't from Edgewater.

On the last day they were there, the men took what looked like a pointy spatula and smoothed cement all over the front of the wall, just like Mom iced her cake. It wasn't until Eugene and Janet went home for dinner that I saw my opportunity.

I made a beeline for Mrs. Cacciotti's wall to figure out how long it was. I began where the wall started and took broad steps around the curve to where it joined Mrs. Mertz's driveway. The whole wall was a total of fifteen big steps. *Perfect!* I thought. *Just exactly what I need.*

I picked up a big stick from Mrs. Mertz's yard, walked back to where the wall started, and drew the top of the first *B* about level with my bangs. I made the two sideways bumps nice and round, ending the bottom one with a fancy curlicue. I took two side steps to the right and drew an *A*. (I had to go back and add a little extra line on the right side to make the legs even.) When I finished the *N* on the far side, facing Mrs. Mertz's, I wiped off my stick on her grass and stepped back to take a good look at my new work of art.

"BARBARA CORCORAN?!" my mother cried as we came upon my masterpiece. "Barbara Ann, what were you thinking?!"

What I was thinking was: *Why couldn't I have just written "Barbara"?* There were lots of Barbaras in Edgewater but only *one* Barbara Corcoran. And that was the one written on Mrs. Cacciotti's wall.

"How could you do that?" my mother scowled, leaning into my face. "And where was your brain? Don't you know if you write your name on a wall, somebody's going to notice?"

I knew it wasn't the kind of question Mom really wanted an answer to. Of course I sort of knew somebody would notice. That was the whole idea. I just didn't know *Mom* was going to notice!

I got sentenced to two weeks of hard labor as Mrs. Cacciotti's slave. I had to knock on her door every morning at eight and say, "Good morning, Mrs. Cacciotti! What can I do for you today?"

I always got the feeling that Mrs. Cacciotti had to think hard to come up with stuff for me to do. But for two weeks I put her milk bottles outside for Mr. Colontoni, the milkman, walked her scrawny brown dog, and swept her front steps. I cleaned up the clippings from her hedges and pulled weeds from her backyard. I didn't like working for Mrs. Cacciotti much, but I was still happy I had written on her wall.

My name was famous on Undercliff Avenue for two whole days! On the third day the workmen came back, and Mom paid them to erase my name from Mrs. Cacciotti's wall.

The Corcoran Group. Getting attention.

I soon learned many ways to write my name on the wall in the crowded New York City market. When I read in every paper that Madonna was pregnant and on the hunt for a new apartment, I immediately sent out a one-page checklist of what Madonna might be looking for. It included the usual things every celebrity wants, like more space, good security, and all the amenities money usually buys. Within hours I was sitting on the set at CNN's studio as the "broker to the stars," chatting up my Madonna report on air. She wasn't my client, but the publicity from that report landed our first celebrity, Richard Gere. It's easy to find ways to tie your business into news that's already out there. It's like hitching your wagon to someone else's horse and going for a free ride.

In today's very corporate climate, firms are often restricted from disclosing spectacular transactions that might prove newsworthy. But there's nothing to stop you from talking about another company's transactions! When a Park Avenue triplex sold for the record-breaking price of $37 million, the selling broker could not talk to the press, so I did! I labeled his $37 million sale a "steal of a deal" that night on *CBS Evening News*, and everyone assumed the biggest deal was mine, while he had to stand on the sidelines and watch.

I learned to use good old-fashioned grandstanding for publicity stunts. When the ridiculous "no dog" pet policies became more common in New York City's snobby co-op buildings, I hired a dog trainer to teach our clients' dogs how to meet and pass the co-op boards. Boards hadn't actually *asked* any dogs to come in for a board interview, but we got our clients' dogs ready anyway. I had a sore back from bending to shake so many doggy paws as photographers snapped away.

There's a little-known American Indian ritual called "smudging," which supposedly chases evil spirits from spaces. When I suggested a smudging to an owner with a hard-to-sell property on Park Avenue to get his property sold, he thought I was out of my mind. But I used it to get four reporters and their cameras out to cover it, and the news coverage it generated sold the property overnight.

16

Sweep the Corners and the Whole House Stays Clean

Summer 1987. The Corcoran Group.

"Okay, ladies," I said, pointing to the list of names on the conference room table and taking in a slow, deep breath. "I know you don't want to fire these people, and I genuinely like each one as much as you do. But the fact remains you've done everything you possibly could for them, and, frankly, these fourteen salespeople will never succeed in the business."

My companions at the conference room table, Esther and our West Side manager, Barbara Brine, gave me a blank look. As in our previous two meetings on the same subject, our discussion was going nowhere. Esther had reluctantly prepared a list ranking our fifty-two salespeople in order of production and was as shocked as I was to see that the top 10 percent of our salespeople were making 80 percent of the company's money. Meanwhile, the bottom 25 percent of our salespeople were draining resources without adding anything back.

Our cost of doing business had climbed along with apartment prices, and our overhead per agent was running $40,000 a year. With the real estate market at a healthy boil, when one agent didn't produce, the next agent's production was big enough to pick up the slack. But I was worried about what would happen if the market braked and slowed to a simmer. Even someone who had failed algebra twice could do the math.

My sales managers had already met with each of their salespeople on the bottom of the list, only to come back and give me a long dissertation on how those who were failing were "really trying their best."

I was stumped and identified with the managers' enormous discomfort. I was asking them to do what I couldn't do myself, and it rendered my order impotent. I found that firing anyone, even when it was the right thing to do, always felt wrong. So lacking the courage to say, "Just fire them," I could only muster, "So, when will you ask them to leave?"

Esther stiffened in her chair, and Barbara looked at the list and sighed. "Four of the bottom ten have never made a deal," Barbara admitted, "but the other six have made almost twenty thousand dollars each and that's certainly better than having an empty desk!"

"No, that's not how it works," I insisted. "With an overhead of forty thousand, that's twenty thousand dollars *short* for each desk! If you multiply *that* times six desks, that's a *hundred and twenty thousand-dollar loss!* We might be in a fat market now and getting away with it, but if the market goes south, we'll be dead on arrival."

What I really wanted to say was: *Listen! I've been talking to you about cleaning up this mess for three months now and nothing has changed! What do I have to do to move this thing along? I won't carry the deadwood any longer. We've got to clean up our mess and we've got to do it now!*

But what I said instead was: "How about we go to the movies?" It seemed the more attainable option.

Esther and Barbara looked bewildered and then relieved. Barbara spoke first: "That sounds like a lovely idea. Doesn't it, Esther?"

We left the office and spent the rest of the afternoon drooling over Mel Gibson in *Lethal Weapon.*

Fall. Hilliard Avenue.

We were halfway up Hilliard Avenue when my older sister, Denise, and I spotted our house through the school bus window. There were lots of colored streamers dangling in the big side-yard tree, and the front retaining wall was draped with dozens of brightly colored flags.

"Whose birthday is it?" Denise asked.

"Don't know," I said, turning and squinting my eyes to get a better look. "Maybe it's Tommy's?"

"Nah, his was last month, but it could be Eddie's. Isn't his after Tommy's?"

"Well, *whosever* birthday it is, it sure looks like Mom outdid herself this time!"

As we neared our house at the top of the hill, the wall decorations began to look less like a party and more like a mess. "De-Denise!" I stammered, nudging her arm and pointing. "Isn't that your new green sweater on the front wall?"

"What!?" she gasped, covering her mouth with both hands.

"Oh, God!" I said, slumping down into the bus seat. "Don't look now, but I think our bras are hanging in the tree!"

By now every kid on the bus had rushed to the left windows, pushing each other aside for a better look. Denise slid down eye level with me and whispered, "It's our clothes, I think maybe all of them—and they're all over the yard!"

"Getting off?" the bus driver shouted back through the catcalls. I grabbed Denise's arm and we made our escape through the accordion doors. "Don't look," I directed through clenched teeth. "Just keep walking straight ahead and pretend we live at the Clearys' house."

"*Nice panties!*" a boy shouted as the bus pulled away. We

walked on, our faces flushed. Denise was swearing under her breath.

"*Who?*" my sister hissed. "*Who* would have done such a *disgusting thing?*"

Together we answered, "*Mom!*"

Mom liked a clean house and surprised us on more than one occasion when she appeared in the girls' room, broom and dustpan in hand, eager to demonstrate her theory on housecleaning.

Mom believed in sweeping corners. First she pulled all the furniture away from the walls and jammed her broom into the nearest corner. Next, she followed the woodwork around clockwise, sweeping the dirt toward the center of the room as she went. Then she pushed the furniture back against the walls, scooped up the dirt pile with her dustpan, and dumped it into a brown paper bag. "Now, remember, girls," she said as she finished a cleaning demonstration, "if you sweep the corners, the whole house stays clean."

When the girls moved upstairs into the new girls' room, Mom made Saturday cleaning *our* responsibility, but we took our extra freedom and ran with it. After we failed Mom's weekly inspections a few times, she began to threaten us with: "If you don't take care of your room in a proper fashion, *I'm* going to take care of it for you!"

Mom had made good on her promise.

———

Denise and I ran up the two flights to our room and surveyed it in horror. Our beds had been stripped. Our blankets were gone, our pillows were gone, and every drawer in our dresser was open and empty. Our room looked as if we had moved out. Only the pink-checked curtains remained, flapping back and forth in the open window.

I walked over and sat down on my bare mattress and reached under it. I was relieved to find my pack of cigarettes undiscovered. "Want a smoke?" I asked Denise as I pulled one out. It was only a filter. I pulled out another, and it was a filter. I dumped out the whole box. Mom had cut every cigarette into thirds and put them, filters up, back in the box. I threw the box across the room into the empty trash can and lay back on my bed.

"Look!" Denise shrieked. I followed her pointing arm. Six-inch letters, scrawled across our dresser mirror in Mom's signature white shoe polish, denounced us as:

PIGS!

"Size eight," I told the woman behind the counter at Celine's Boutique, on Park Avenue. We were walking back from *Lethal Weapon* when I spotted the pink suede shoes in the store window. The shoes must have been for the woman who had everything. They had little pink bunny ears attached to the front, a set of rolling glass eyes beneath curly black lashes, and a black sculpted nose with a set of long bunny whiskers.

"That will be two hundred and twenty-two dollars, please," the woman behind the counter said. Esther and Barbara looked at me as if I had lost my mind as I wrote out the check.

When I got back to the office, I removed my new bunny shoes from their box and placed them on my desk. I took out the list of nonproductive salespeople and reached for a cube of paper.

"H.H.," I wrote on the first small yellow square.

"A.Z.," I wrote on the next.

"S.K.," I wrote on the one after that and continued until all ten of the salespeople's initials were written on individual squares. I folded the papers in half, then in quarters, and then in eighths. I dropped five of the tiny notes in each shoe, placed the bunnies back in their box, and taped my handwritten note to Barbara Brine on top. It read:

BB:

Ask these people to hop on

out of here by <u>Friday</u>!

   —Barb

    xx

I sealed the box and sent it by messenger to the West Side office.

Within an hour of getting the shoes, Barbara called, laughing. She said she'd "hop right to it," and that afternoon, she fired her first unproductive salesperson.

With the bunny shoes I succeeded in making the dreadful topic of firing a bit friendlier and gave the sales managers the courage to set needed deadlines. The $222 bunny shoes saved The Corcoran Group $120,000 that year, as the money was no longer being spent to support nonproductive salespeople.

17

In a Family, Everyone Helps
Mash the Potatoes

Spring 1989. New York City.

We had just signed a new lease for five thousand fancy feet
of space on Madison Avenue when the stock market crashed in
October '87. Black Monday sent the economy into a tailspin and
real estate into a free fall.

Things only got worse. By the spring of 1989, after a year
and a half of juggling our finances and begging our creditors for
more time, our bills were piling up faster than our commissions.
Putting deals together had become an impossible task. I had to
agree with Esther when she said she wished we had some cash
reserves.

———

Esther had our bills laid out in stacks on the conference room table. Her neatly written note on top read, "Barb, you better have a look."

I sat down and riffled through the piles. The biggest stack was from the advertising agency. It stood eight inches high and totaled more than $100,000. I was happy to note that per my instruction, both the office rent and the payroll were paid to date, but according to my quick calculation, we owed another $200,000 for printing, office supplies, equipment leases, insurance, accounting fees, and telephone. I added up our accounts receivable, and if our deals closed within the next four months as projected, our net commissions would total only $36,000.

"Whew," I gasped, shaking the number out of my head. "That leaves us with a shortfall of $264,000!" I pulled the tape from the adding machine, circled the red figure, walked to my desk, and hid it in my file drawer.

When I reached for my purse, I found a note clipped to it. It read, "Don't forget we have the $300,000 credit line at Citibank. Esther."

Dad's La-Z-Boy. Edgewater.

Mom was in her usual rush down the rickety wooden stairs, which led from the bathroom to the cellar, when she took a bad fall and broke her ankle in two places. She was on her way to check the furnace, which kicked off whenever the Roanes filled their tub at the same time we did. She was trying to get down and back before the breaded veal patties burned in the frying pan.

Even with her leg in a cast, Mom kept charging at full throttle. She hopped up and down the front steps on her good leg, almost as fast as we ran them on two. She had a wheelchair, a walker, crutches, and, most important, another foot.

Mom altered her daily routines to accommodate the new annoyance and used her walker as a temporary clothesline, draping things over it as if it were a drying rack. She discovered that by wrapping the heel of her crutch with a damp rag and a rubber band, she could reach into the tight spots to clean out the cobwebs. Her wheelchair soon sat parked in the side yard, where it served as a temporary stool for peeling potatoes.

Mom's new condition didn't change Dad's routine at all. Each night before leaving for his second job as night watchman at the Lever Brothers Company, Dad still settled into his La-Z-Boy chair in the living room for his evening smoke. He opened his tin of Half and Half tobacco, took a large pinch, and carefully stuffed his burled-wood pipe. After a few puffs, he leaned back, rested his pipe on a beanbag ashtray, cocked his head back, and fell asleep. That was Dad's routine, and that's where he sat the night Mom lost it.

It was shortly before dinner and Mom was crutching around

the kitchen, hopping back and forth between the sink, refrigerator, and stove. Baby Jeanine was on her hip and Marty Joe was pulling at her hem. Ellen and I were setting the table.

Mom finished draining the potatoes and dumped them and a stick of butter into her big aluminum pot. She hopped over to the refrigerator, took out the milk, and poured some into the potatoes. With her free hand, she stuck the Sunbeam mixer into the potatoes and turned it on. The pot whirled around once, twice, and then spun right off the counter and onto the floor.

Chunks of potatoes whirled through the kitchen. Marty Joe started to laugh, smearing the potatoes through his hair and into his ears. I looked at Mom, and she looked as if she were about to cry.

"EDDIEEE!" she screamed at the top of her lungs. "EDDIE, HELP ME!"

Dad jerked his head up from the back of his La-Z-Boy and stammered, "What? . . . What, what is it, Florence?"

Mom hobbled over to the La-Z-Boy, her hair glued to her forehead with sweat. Ellen and I stood frozen at the end of the table. We looked at each other, then at Mom, and back to Dad. Mom spoke slowly through clenched teeth. "Can, you, please, come, here, and, do *something*?"

"Like what, Flo?" Dad answered.

"Like, maybe, help, me, mash, the, damn, *potatoes*!"

"Florence," Dad replied, "you know that's not my job."

Dad picked up his pipe and Mom hopped back to the kitchen.

When Esther wrote the first check against our credit line, we discovered it had been pulled by Mr. Serling, our ex–friendly banker. He explained that credit lines were really for businesses that didn't need credit.

I knew something had to give, and it wasn't going to be Citibank.

Two silver-haired Italian men dressed in dark gray hand-stitched suits arrived at my office and introduced themselves as Mr. Vincent Albanese and Mr. Tony Albanese. They had built a new fifty-two-story condominium across from the United Nations and had blueprints rolled under their arms. They sat down in my small eleventh-floor office and the older brother, Vincent, commented on its neatness. "Small, but beautifully kept," he said.

Tony, the younger brother, seemed like the dealmaker. "My brother and I read your comments in yesterday's *Times*," he began, "and my brother and I are wondering if you'd be so kind as to tell us what you think our new condominium apartments could sell for."

"I'd be more than happy to, Mr. and Mr. Albanese," I replied, my mind warming at the thought of the commission on

250 apartments. "If you can take the time now to walk me through your blueprints, I can have prices for you by tomorrow."

When they left, I unrolled their floor plans and walked out to the sales area. "Linda," I interrupted a salesperson, "would you take a quick look at these apartment plans and give me your best guess as to what each might sell for?" Linda did; I wrote her initials next to each of her estimates and then moved on to the next salesperson.

Forty-five minutes later, I had collected ten opinions. After averaging the prices for each of the six apartment sizes, I had a pretty good idea what the Albaneses' condominiums would sell for.

The two brothers arrived the next morning, and they seemed impressed by the neatly typed list of prices I had prepared. "Excellent work," Vincent congratulated me, as he examined the list of prices. "Excellent work!"

During the next few minutes of back-and-forth schmoozing, all I could think about was the $264,000 that I owed to my creditors. We needed cash and we needed it now. I decided to go for it.

"Mr. Albanese and Mr. Albanese, I've never in my entire life seen more beautiful floor plans than yours. They reflect the enormous thought you've obviously put into every detail. Your building's location is exceptional, your views the best in the city, and your black marble pyramid top is going to put the Empire State Building to shame! *I just love your building*, Mr. Albaneses, and I wonder if you would consider giving The Corcoran Group the honor of selling your property as your exclusive agent?" I bowed my head with respect and waited.

The brothers looked at each other, obviously impressed by my appreciation of their trophy property. It was Vincent who finally spoke, almost painfully. "Unfortunately, Miss Corcoran, I'm sorry to say that it's out of the question! Marty Raynes is a partner in our project and his company is already our exclusive agent."

I thought again about the $264,000. I thought about the credit line that got away. And I thought about this week's sales, which totaled only two.

I smiled my most innocent smile.

"Well, how about sales manager?" I asked, trying to disguise my desperation as enthusiasm.

Tony smiled like a kindly godfather, and asked, "But why would *you*, Miss Corcoran, want to work as a sales manager when you're the president of this successful operation?"

"Because I could learn so much working for you and your brother," I explained. Tony seemed satisfied with my answer and leaned back.

Vincent, however, was suspicious, squinting his eyes and pursuing the question further. "I think that might be a conflict of interest," he said. "Let's say, Miss Corcoran, that one of your salespeople brought in a customer who bought one of our condos. We would owe your company a full 5 percent commission.

How could I be sure that that customer didn't come into our building first, and that you didn't refer him to one of your salespeople just to get the commission?"

At that, I spread my hand over my heart and gasped. I remembered my "almost a nun" statement, which had worked so well years earlier with Mr. Campagna, my landlord who wanted to evict me. I decided right then to take the story one step further.

"Mr. Albaneses, *that* would be impossible! Why, I'm a former nun!"

I started work with the respectful Italian Albanese brothers one week later for an annual salary of $200,000. I planned to use half of my new salary to pay Esther so that she could give up sales and be in the office full-time. I'd use the other $100,000 to keep ahead on our advertising bill. If we couldn't advertise our listings, we'd be out of business.

In the second week on my new job, a sophisticated Italian woman arrived at the condominium sales office. She looked a lot like Sophia Loren, and I knew she was a "ringer," a spy to test my integrity. She might as well have been carrying a sign.

"I've beena working, witha Eleanora, froma Tha Corcoran Groupa," she tolda mea. "Do I needa, hera, to showa-mea, thesa condos?"

"Why, that's not necessary at all," I replied. "I'll take you up to see the condos right now." She didn't buy a condo, but I had honored my vows and passed the Albanese integrity test.

I thought back to my memory of my mother quietly hopping back to the kitchen as my dad sat in his La-Z-Boy. Mom's unspoken words still echoed in my memory: "In a family, *everyone helps mash the potatoes.*"

For the next six months, I fed my after-tax income back to The Corcoran Group, earning the needed cash that bought my struggling company some time. And I discovered that the new job gave me the opportunity to learn something new, and through that job, I learned a lot about marketing new developments. That knowledge would later lead to the opening of a new marketing division for The Corcoran Group.

My willingness to go out and take a second job to keep us afloat set an example that was noticed by everyone at the company. Because I was willing to personally put myself on the line, everyone at The Corcoran Group rallied around the flag and pitched in. They formed listing teams, taught workshops, helped each other negotiate, supported cuts in advertising, and even took pay cuts.

Nothing is more powerful than a team working together. Teams can accomplish anything, but to create an exceptional team, the members must totally believe that *not one of us is as smart as all of us.*

18

Moms Can't Quit

December 1990. The Corcoran Group.

Every time the office door opened, I looked up from my desk with dread. I was petrified that someone would walk in with a big dolly and walk out with our furniture. I hadn't taken a salary from the business in months and with the help of a friendly mortgage broker had put a $450,000 mortgage on my $350,000 country house. That money was already spent so I sold my third-floor one-bedroom condo on East 63rd Street and moved one block down into an illegal sublet, a rent-controlled walk-up on East 62nd, which was leased by my cousin.

My new apartment came with a pet, the biggest cockroach

in New York City, and he lived in my bathtub. When I got home at night, he was there waiting for me, wiggling his two antennae back and forth above the drain. I surprised myself by taking a liking to him, and soon considered him my pet.

In recent months, the only phone ringing belonged to Sylvia, my secretary-bookkeeper, and she had clearly become the most popular person at the office. She answered one call after another from suppliers, offering small goodwill payments in exchange for a little more time.

Esther suggested I use her personal savings to keep the business afloat, and one of my nicest salespeople, Edith, quietly offered me her husband's pension fund. But not knowing if I would be able to pay either back, I declined. I felt bad enough owing our creditors money, never mind owing money to people I knew personally.

I went over our bills and receivables once more. We were clearly in the red, blood red, and for the first time, I faced the fact that we were going out of business.

I unplugged the office Christmas tree, turned off the lights, and headed home through the holiday hustle of Madison Avenue. I needed to find the right words to tell everyone I was closing the business, but I figured I could wait two weeks, until after the holidays.

Friday night. The Corcoran kitchen.

"I quit!" Mom declared to no one as the kitchen filled with smoke, and she clanged the smoking black pan of charred flounder into the sink. She stomped over to Dad's La-Z-Boy and handed Mary Jean off with a curt "She's wet; change her!"

The next time we saw Mom it was almost six o'clock. We were milling around the kitchen when she appeared in her full Sunday dress, hat and all. Nana was standing on her right, and her blue Samsonite suitcase was at the ready on her left.

"I'm leaving!" she announced loudly.

"What about dinner?" Eddie asked.

"Your father's in charge. Ask him!" she said, picking up her suitcase and heading toward the front door.

We all ran to the front window to watch Mom ka-thump her suitcase down the front steps, jerk it up onto the sidewalk, and head down Hilliard Avenue. We watched as she dragged her suitcase past Gene's candy store, Mrs. Mertz's bakery, Bernie Beck's supermarket, and as she went over the ridge by Uncle Dick's police station, we couldn't see Mom anymore.

Mom plunked herself down on the green wooden bench at the bus stop on River Road and waited. She didn't know where she was going; she was just going. With a household full of kids, Mom was tired of being the full-time repairman, laundress, nurse, tutor, and cook. But the final straw that Friday night was that Dad wasn't helping her get us ready for his cousin's wedding the next day in Toms River.

As she waited for the number 8 bus to New York, a handsome, well-dressed man with a leather attaché case sat down next to her. Mom yanked the two pink sponge curlers from her bangs. When the bus arrived, she paid her fare and took a seat at the front, and the handsome man sat down beside her. "Going my way?" he whispered to my mother.

It was two blocks south at the stop in front of the Edgewater Aluminum Factory that Mom grabbed her suitcase and ran off of the bus.

We were all sitting at the dinner table, pushing Nana's frozen fish sticks around our plates, when Mom appeared in the kitchen. "I'm home," she said to no one, and plunked her suitcase down.

We looked up at Mom and waited. John was the first to ask, "Where'd you go, Mom?"

"To the aluminum factory and back," she said, taking off her hat.

"But Dad said you quit," Ellen added, taking a quick look at Dad.

Mom sat down, sprinkled some peas onto Mary Jean's tray, and said, "Moms can't quit."

———

I find that every big success happens after I think I've exhausted 100 percent of my options. For me, success happened only *after* I gave another 10 percent. After trying everything to keep my business afloat, I returned to the office on January 2, and received one of the most challenging and timely phone calls of my life.

19

When There Are Ten Buyers and Three Puppies, Every Dog Is the Pick of the Litter

Early January 1991.

I had already scheduled the sales meeting to announce the closing of the business when a big developer called and asked that I appraise a group of eighty-eight apartments in six buildings that he and his financial partners owned on the Upper East and West sides. The apartments were leftovers from the go-go years, before the real estate market did a jackknife dive and ended with a splat.

Bernie Mendik and his investment partner, Equitable Insurance, had a $50 million underlying mortgage on the buildings, leaving each apartment's monthly maintenance charge 40 percent higher than that of the rest of the market. The high maintenance, along with the difficulty buyers were having in finding financing, made the apartments virtually impossible to sell.

I took a trip over to look at these apartments that had languished on the market for three years with no takers. One after one, I previewed them, each as dreadful as the last. "Where's the kitchen?" I asked as the superintendent opened the door to yet another one.

"This one doesn't have one," he said, "but the pipes are all there."

I looked at the white-tile, white-tub, white-sinked bathroom badly in need of caulking. "At least there's a bathroom!" I commented, and closed the door.

Finding buyers for these apartments would be impossible. Prices had plummeted 40 percent since the stock market crashed in '87, and every would-be customer in New York City thought that if they waited, they'd be able to buy the apartment for less the following day.

I returned to the office and called Mr. Mendik. "I'm afraid I have bad news, Bernie," I began. "There's just no way your apartments can be sold in this market. They've been listed for more than three years and there aren't any takers. I'm sure you're aware that the apartments need a ton of work and the maintenance charges are way out of line with the rest of the market. I'm sorry, Bernie, I really wish I could help."

"Barbara," Bernie responded with his trademark enthusiasm, "you're a smart girl! You'll figure it out." And he hung up the phone.

Summer. Toms River.

Grandpa Ward was a huge man with big hands who lived in a small clapboard cabin in Toms River, New Jersey. To visit him, we took the two-hour trip sardine-style in the back of Dad's Blue Beauty station wagon. Grandpa Ward's house was at the end of a long dirt road, which he shared with the chicken farmer across the way.

When we arrived, Grandpa had already prepared the usual lunch of warmed canned beets that he insisted were rich in iron and guaranteed to make my brothers "strong, strappin' men." My sisters and I quietly wondered if women got strappin', and if not, why did we have to eat them, too?

We were sitting outside on Grandpa's screened porch after lunch when I heard a lot of noise at the farm across the road. "MOM!" I yelled with my hands cupped on the screen door. "There's some fancy cars pulling up to the farm. Can we go see what's going on?"

"Just a minute," she answered, "and we'll all go together.

Ellen, help me finish the dishes, and, Denise, put away the cups. John, sit on Grandpa's lap there and, Eddie, wipe your face. Barbara, stay right there, and keep your eye on Tommy, Mary, Martin, and Jeanine."

By the time we got to the road, there was a line of fancy cars, and a line of fancy city folks to go with them waited by the gate.

"What's going on today?" my mother asked a lady in a very shiny dress.

"What's going on?" the lady repeated, flapping a fan in front of her face. "What's going on is that that farmer lady gave me an appointment at noon and then let *that* woman there ahead of me."

"I had an appointment at noon, too," grumbled the bald-headed man behind her.

"And so did *we*," a very skinny lady said, standing with a man by their blue convertible. "And, by the way," the very skinny lady added, "you're behind *us*."

"Oh, I don't have an appointment," my mother explained, as she straightened the hem of her housedress. "We're just visiting our relatives next door."

"What's everyone waiting for?" Denise asked.

"For the puppies," the lady with the fan said as if we should know. "They're Jack Russells, and they have three of them for sale right over there next to the barn."

"You better make that *two*," a lady with a poufed head of

blond hair said as she walked past cradling a tiny brown-spotted puppy. She was making baby sounds. "I got the absolutely cutest one of all! Just look at his sweet little face!"

The people waiting in line bristled, and Mom moved us out of the way as the line squeezed closer together. "Come over here, kids," she directed, as the fan lady hurried through the gate, "and I'll tell you what's really going on." Mom laughed to herself as she explained: "The farmer's wife was smart enough to get everyone to come at the same time because she knew it would make everyone want a puppy!"

"But why would it make everyone want a puppy, Mom?" Ellen asked.

"Because everybody wants what everybody wants. And when there are ten buyers and only three puppies, every dog becomes the pick of the litter."

I had an idea! What was good for the puppies would be good for apartments. The next day, I called Bernie back to make an appointment. Bernie liked my new idea and asked me to explain it to his partners later that week, which I did. Next, I explained it to three serious men from the underwriting banks. And later I explained it to the even *more* serious men from the lead lender, Chase Manhattan Bank. And finally I explained it to the *most* serious men of all, from the Equitable Life Insurance Society of the United States, the majority investor. They all seriously liked it.

By the fifteenth of January, my last-ditch plan to save my business was in full swing.

"Here's how it works," I said to Esther and to one of my best agents, Tresa Hall. Tresa had agreed to be the project's sales manager. "I've priced all the studios at $49,500, all the one-bedrooms at $99,500, and all the two-bedrooms at $165,500."

"Even the high floors?" Esther interrupted.

"Yes, high floors, low floors, front apartments and back apartments, *all priced the same*. Apartments with views or no views, those with new kitchens, old kitchens, or no kitchens at all, all priced the same!"

"But how's that possible?" Esther asked.

"I added up all of the original asking prices, divided by the number of units in each building, and then deducted 10 percent, because that's what people would have negotiated off the price anyway."

Esther shifted slightly in her chair.

"And I've also taken away every objection that a buyer could possibly have. There's no board approval needed and one of the banks with a big stake in the buildings has agreed to provide the mortgages. Also, there'll be no monthly maintenance charges for *two whole years*! None!"

"*None?*" Tresa repeated. "But that's crazy! Who'll pay the maintenance each month?"

"The sellers will," I answered, "because it's included in the sale price. We're simply giving the buyers one less check to write each month and moving the high-maintenance objection out of the way." I pulled out a sample contract and continued, "We'll have the eighty-eight contracts prepared in advance by the seller's attorney, and we'll stack them high for everyone to see. The buyers will sign them right then and there the morning of the sale."

"But that isn't legal, is it?" Esther queried, as she tilted her head to the left. "Barbara, you know buyers have to show the contract to their attorney before they can sign it!"

I pulled out the big rubber stamp I had had made and with one quick motion imprinted the sample contract on my desk with bold lettering:

> **<u>CONSULT YOUR ATTORNEY.</u>**
> **YOU HAVE TWO WEEKS FROM THIS**
> **DATE TO CANCEL THE CONTRACT AND**
> **RECEIVE YOUR FULL DEPOSIT BACK.**

Esther and Tresa looked cautiously optimistic.

At the next Monday meeting, I announced to our salespeople that we had eighty-eight new co-op apartments for sale, that they were located in six different buildings on the Upper East and West sides, and that we were going to sell all of the apartments on the same day for the same price. "Pick any studio for $49,500," I said emphatically, "any one-bedroom for $99,500, or any two-bedroom for $165,500!"

When I wouldn't disclose the apartments' addresses, everyone wanted to know where they were even more. "This is not a sale open to *everyone* and it will *not* be advertised." I had no money for advertising, but didn't share that fact. "We will distribute the exact addresses and unit numbers *only* on the morning of the sale. I ask that you please tell only, I repeat *only*, your very best customers. And, of course, you can also tell your family. The sale is limited to *one per customer* and will take place three weeks from today, first come, first served. Nine A.M. sharp!"

Everyone looked intrigued, and after I ended the meeting, I could still hear the buzz from my office.

Two weeks before the day of the sale, I added fuel to the fire by worrying aloud to a few salespeople, "I'm a little concerned that we might not have enough to go around." My whisper campaign created a virtual frenzy.

A week before the sale, accusations began to fly that someone had gotten hold of "the list" and that she was already telling her customers which apartments were the best ones. I quelled the rumor at that Monday's meeting.

"No one has the list!" I stated emphatically to the crowded sales floor. "I repeat, no one has the list! There's *only one list*, and it's safely locked in Esther Kaplan's drawer. Esther, please show them!" With that, Esther played magician's assistant and walked over to her desk, where she unlocked the drawer and pulled out the sheets of typed paper. As she held them up and turned from one side of the room to the other, fifty salespeople wiggled forward for a better view.

"Thank you, Esther." I nodded. "Now, please lock it back up!" Everyone watched as Esther put the list into an envelope, put the envelope in the drawer, locked it, and dropped the key into her purse. "*Everyone* will get the list next Monday morning, nine A.M. sharp!"

8:55 A.M. *East 69th Street.*

"Stand back!" Tresa Hall, a former flight attendant, commanded the chaotic, shoving throng of buyers. "I repeat, stand back and clear the doors!"

I was shocked to see the crowd of buyers stretching to the end of the block. "Excuse me, excuse me, please, excuse me," I repeated as I made my way up East 69th Street.

The line had started at four A.M., and by eight thirty had grown to include hundreds of people desperate to snag an apartment. Tresa's voice cut through the crowd. "We will distribute the list of apartments momentarily," she said, demonstrating with broad flight attendant arm motions. "And we'll be handing it out starting in the front and will work our way to the back of the line as quickly as possible. Please note that a map is attached to the back of each list with all the addresses and apartment numbers clearly marked. There are salespeople stationed on every floor in each of the buildings; the apartment doors are open, so that you can go in and look at any apartment you choose. Once you've made your decision, however, you must return to *this* table in *this* lobby to sign the contract." She directed all eyes toward the banquet table, which stood in the lobby with eighty-eight waiting contracts stacked high.

"When you are ready to sign a contract and leave us your 10 percent deposit check, the apartment will be *immediately* taken off the market. Please have several apartments you'd like to try for, as your first choice may already be taken! You'll be given a copy of the signed contract to take with you for your attorney.

"Okay, then," Tresa finished, and with great ceremony said, "we'll now hand out the list of apartments!" The crowd lunged forward and I wondered if I should have hired a few uniformed policemen to protect her, or at least for dramatic effect.

As in a Macy's One Day Sale without the clothes, people began to run the moment the list was in their hands. In the mayhem, everyone had a strategy for charting, hunting, darting, looking, rushing, signing, and buying. Some people waited on elevators, while others bolted for the stairs. Some worked alone; others worked in pairs.

The first successful buyer had flown in from Paris and had camped in line since four o'clock that morning. He signed a contract for a one-bedroom on the highest floor, sight unseen, six blocks away.

One savvy couple had a pair of cellular phones and were calling each other back and forth as they dashed through the buildings looking at apartments. It was the first time I saw cell phones in use. When they decided on an apartment they liked, the husband ran to the table while his wife kept looking, just in case. As he signed the contract, he called his wife on her cellular and said, "Honey, we got one; you can stop."

One man rushed back to the contract table announcing he liked the C line of apartments in the building. "It doesn't matter which floor; I just want to buy a C, any C." When we told him that all the C's had been sold, he decided he liked B's, too, "any B."

We started the day with eighty-eight apartments that nobody had wanted and our company near bankruptcy. By day's end, eighty-eight proud new owners were celebrating their good fortune, and we had eighty-eight checks to deposit and had earned more than a million dollars in net commissions. The Corcoran Group would live to see another day.

20

Jumping Out the Window Will Make You Either an Ass or a Hero

1993. The Corcoran Group.

For the first time in a long time, I had ended the previous year with a profit, a clear $71,000 after-tax profit, and it was burning a hole in my pocket. I knew God had put that money in my hand for some divine purpose, and I had already decided to spend all of it on my amazing new video idea.

I hired a photographer to take pictures of our listings—seventy-three, to be exact—and put them on videotape. The videos were categorized by the number of bedrooms and featured the floor plans, the building's lobby, and even the views outside the windows. Each listing description ended with a photo and the phone number of the listing salesperson. I even hired a professional makeup artist so our salespeople would look their very best.

I couldn't wait to introduce my new idea at the company-wide sales meeting! I stood at the lit podium in front of my two hundred or so salespeople and bragged, "Our new videos will give our Corcoran Group customers *all the information* they could possibly want. All in one convenient place! We're calling it *Homes on Tape. HOT* for short. Get it? Now, thanks to this innovation, our customers can shop for apartments anywhere, anytime, simply by picking up a copy of our video at any of our offices and taking it home for only a twenty-dollar, fully refundable deposit. It's just perfect for the busy New Yorker!"

As I raised my arms into a high papal V, I vowed, "Our *Homes on Tape* will transform the way people buy and sell real estate forever! Now New Yorkers will be able to see all the property they want, without ever having to leave their own couch! Amen!"

The entire sales team burst into spontaneous applause as I dramatically nodded my head and lowered my arms. *Yep*, I thought, *this is my best idea yet!*

Summer. The side yard.

Marty Joe was perched on the ledge of the third-story window outside the girls' room, grinning from ear to ear. "*We're ready!*" we all shouted up.

Marty's legs looked white against his navy blue swim trunks high above our heads. He was about to leap out over the Roanes' landing into the plastic, metal-framed pool Dad and Grandpa had set up in the side yard. The pool was four feet deep, but was a lot shallower next to the house, where Dad and Grandpa couldn't make it level against the hill.

"*Are you sure you're ready?*" Marty shouted down. For a moment, I thought he looked nervous, maybe even scared, but Marty Joe was the kid who would try anything.

"Come on, let's *go*, Marty Joe!" Jimmy Cleary called up.

"Do it, Dart!" another kid added.

My brother Marty had more nicknames than any other member of our family. He was baptized Martin Joseph, which had been shortened to Marty Joe. Later, the kids in the neighborhood named him Martin Jartin. That lasted until the summer day when he demonstrated his technique for throwing a dart in the air and catching it by its tail. Blinded by the glare of the sun, he missed a dart as it shot back to earth, and it landed smack between his eyes.

The other kids' excited cries as they watched him run in circles like a chicken without a head were music to Marty's attention-loving ears. "Look at me!" he shouted to the crowd like the sideshow barker at the amusement park. "Look at me, the aa-maaaazing Martin *Dart*in, pierced by a flying dart that went straight to his *braaaaaaaain*!"

With the bloody dart poking from his forehead like a bull's-eye shot on a dartboard, Marty took a bow to mixed applause and shrieks of horror. His self-anointed name stuck, and Martin Jartin became forever known as Martin Dartin, or Dart for short.

"Dart," Michael Mertz shouted up with his hands cupped like a megaphone, "we don't have all day!"

With that, Martin Dartin leapt off the window ledge, sailed past Mrs. Roane's landing, and hurtled toward the shallow section of our plastic pool.

"What an asshole!" my brother Eddie shouted, as we all scrambled away from the pool with a collective gasp. I covered my eyes as Marty plunged into the water. When I opened them, Marty was standing up in the middle of the pool bowing, and everyone ran and crowded around the pool.

"I don't believe it! I don't believe it! I just don't believe it," we all clamored, congratulating Marty for being alive.

Marty seemed as amazed by his survival as we were. Shaking the water from his hair, he reached out for the hands of his adoring fan club.

"Hey, what's happening?" Stevie Mertz hollered as he hurdled our front retaining wall. "What's going on, what did I miss?"

"Dart just jumped off the roof and lived!" Timmy Tom proudly exclaimed as he inched closer to Marty, trying to catch some of his afterglow.

"And he hit the pool dead center!" Ellen bragged.

"Oh, man," Stevie whined, "but I didn't see it. That's a bummer."

Without a moment's thought, Marty gripped the pool's edge, swung his muscular legs between his arms, and popped out of the pool, dripping wet. "No problem!" he said. "Watch me this time; I'll do it again."

Before Marty's second jump ended, he had already become the town hero.

That night, while Mom pounded the chicken cutlets, we were all still talking about Marty's amazing feat. Mom didn't look happy. She rolled out a sheet of waxed paper, looked up at Marty, and said, "You know, Marty, jumping out a window can make you either an ass *or* a hero. You just got *lucky*." As Dad came in the front door from work, Mom lowered her voice. "Since your father's interpretation won't match your friends'," she warned, pointing with the meat cleaver, "you better keep your braggin' to yourself."

December 1993. Corcoran West Side.

I made my way down the wooden steps that leaned precariously against the moldy cinder-block wall in the wet basement of our West Side office, right next door to Zabar's deli on Broadway.

I pulled the string on the single lightbulb at the bottom of the stairs, and it cast a dull yellow light over the final resting place of my $71,000 investment. Thirty-two piles of black video boxes were stacked eight feet high against the back wall. My *Homes on Tape* idea had been dead on arrival, and not one person had come to check out our video sales tour.

My brilliant marketing innovation had a pair of Achilles' heels. First, our salespeople wouldn't give out the videos because they didn't want to show customers another salesperson's face or phone number. Second, the videos contained so many images that each shot clicked on and off faster than even the New York eye could possibly see.

I glared at the eight-foot pile of videos sucking up the water from the basement floor and knew I should be giving some serious thought to how to recoup the $71,000 I had blown on my big idea. But instead all I could think about was the next big sales meeting and how stupid I would look standing there in front of everyone explaining why my great idea had belly-flopped.

I climbed back up the basement stairs and headed over to the East Side, where I was meeting my husband at Maxwell's Plum for dinner. A former FBI agent and a captain in the naval reserves, Wild Bill Higgins had just returned from three weeks of war games with the U.S. Navy in South Korea. He was anxious to tell me about his trip and, between big bites of steak, he excitedly gestured and explained how he had played war games against North Korea on computer. He was a lot more animated than usual.

"It was incredible, Barb; you should have seen it! We fought the whole war on this new thing called the Internet, and it was exactly like a *real war*. We were moving our ships and supplies as if there was really a war going on!"

I was still bruised by the soggy image of my pile of tapes and was trying my best to feign interest. I took another sip of my white wine and said, "Didn't you play those same games last year in Washington?"

"It was totally different, Barb." He chewed on. "We were actually playing war in *real time*. When the North Koreans bombed us, we immediately bombed them back. And when they took out our ports and highways, we instantly blew up their supply ships. You could see everything on the computer like it was actually happening!"

"Well, who won?" I asked, hoping to conclude and move on to my subject.

He smiled. "*They* did!" he said. "And the South Koreans went berserk! You'd think they had actually lost a war." He gestured with his fork. "We had to keep reminding them that it was just a game on a computer!"

"Is the Internet thing only in the Navy?" I asked. "Made to play war games?"

"No, Barb, that's just it; it's not just for games. Anyone can use it to exchange any information with anyone, anywhere, any-time, as long as they have a computer. And it's free! I'm telling you, Barb, this World Wide Web is going to connect everybody and become the greatest library of instant information on the planet!"

The following week, my salesperson Linda Stillwell volunteered to have her husband in the computer business register our com-pany's "domain" name on his computer. Then I hired the video guy to put our *Homes on Tape* pictures on the World Wide Web.

January 1994.

"Ladies and gentlemen, today I'm proud to announce phase two of our *Homes on Tape* video project! The Corcoran Group will be one of the first companies in America to take our listings into cyberspace!" Although I didn't know if anyone besides the South Koreans could *find* our listings there, I knew for sure that I had come up with a plan to save face. Everyone applauded.

Within the month, four new customers found our properties on the World Wide Web, and my belly flop began to look like a heroic leap into the future.

21

You Have the Right to Be There

December 1993. The Corcoran Group.

It all started when my assistant, Sylvia, bustled into my office, her feathers obviously ruffled. "She says her name is Susan Cara and she's one of our salespeople," Sylvia puffed, "but *I've* never seen her before, and she doesn't even have an appointment!"

"That's okay, Sylvia," I said, smoothing her feathers. "Just show her in."

Susan Cara had the best legs I'd ever seen on *anyone*. She clicked over to my desk in heels so high I got ready to catch her if she tripped. The micro-mini she wore was a half inch too short and I could see she didn't have stockings on. She tugged her skirt down as she slid into the chair across from my desk and grinned, the tip of her tongue resting on her two front teeth.

"It's nice to meet you, Susan," I said. "Sylvia tells me you're one of our new salespeople."

"I'm not new," she corrected me.

"Oh, I'm sorry," I apologized. "I haven't met you before, so I assumed you were new. How long have you been here?"

"Three weeks."

"Three weeks," I repeated. "Well, I guess that seems like a long time." I settled in for what I knew was going to be an interesting conversation. "So, how can I help you?"

Susan crossed her legs once and then again in the other direction. "I have an investor," she started, "and he wants to buy big hotels in New York."

"Oh, that's good news," I said. "I can certainly help you with that. I'll call the two largest commercial firms and get you the name of their best broker who specializes in hotel sales. Who's your customer?"

"A conglomerate," she answered abruptly.

"Okay, then, Susan," I said, "you don't have to give me the name, but you should know that you'll have to give *them* your customer's name if you want to collect a referral commission. They'll probably pay you 20 or maybe even 25 percent of their commission, and on a hotel sale that could be sizable."

Susan leaned forward in her seat. "No," she said firmly. "I plan to sell them myself."

"Susan, although I can appreciate that, you've only been with us for three weeks, so you might not know that the commercial sales business is a whole different kettle of fish than residential sales. Our company sells apartments and town houses, because that's our expertise. I'm afraid you'd be doing yourself, our company, and, most important, your *customer* a disservice if you tried to help them yourself. But if you refer them, you'll have the best two commercial firms in New York working for your customer."

"Thank you." She smiled and left my office to go out and totally ignore my advice.

"I'm telling you, Barbara, this lady is going to get us in trouble," Susan's sales manager fretted to me by phone. "She's calling every big hotel owner in town, asking them to sell their property to her mystery client, and leaving a wake of complaints in her path. She has absolutely no idea what she's talking about, and she won't listen. I think you should do something about her, Barbara, because everything about her spells trouble."

Susan's manager told me she had hired her because Susan was very aggressive and seemed eager to learn. But within her few short weeks at the company, she had succeeded in alienating the entire office; the others saw her as different and resented her know-it-all attitude.

Her manager reported that Susan wasn't interested in learning her real estate ABC's. She knew exactly what she wanted, which was to jump from A to Z. And she got lucky by snagging a big conglomerate referral when she listed her own house for sale in Brooklyn.

I waited two days to get an appointment, and when she finally prowled into my office, it was clear to me that I was either going to have to fire her or let her do exactly as she pleased.

"So, Susan, how's it going?" I pleasantly inquired.

"I want you to call Donald Trump for me," she answered. "My client wants to buy the Plaza Hotel."

"Ohkaaay," I said. "But you need to tell me something about your client, Susan."

"Like what?" she asked.

"Like where he's from," I said.

"Hong Kong," she aggressively snapped back.

"And *who* exactly are they?" I persisted.

"A conglomerate."

"Listen, Susan, I need to know more than that. I'll need to know that they're legitimate buyers before I can make any calls for you."

"They're for real," she stated conclusively, looking around the room as if I were wasting her time.

At the last toss of her hair, I was beginning to relish the thought of firing her. I leaned back in my chair, trying to arrive at the right solution.

I tried to put my dislike for Susan aside and had to acknowledge that anyone who was so dogged in holding on to a client probably *did* have a big fish on the end of the line. And by witnessing how aggressive she was, I figured she would somehow find a way to reel it in.

But I knew I couldn't have Susan running around town alienating the commercial property owners and risking my reputation in the process. Susan was way out of her league. She didn't know a damn thing about selling commercial property. In fact, Susan and The Corcoran Group had no right whatsoever dabbling in someone else's market.

Spring. Chicky Dayock's house.

"Barbara Ann," Mom said, "Chicky Dayock is a very nice woman, and you have nothing to be afraid of. Besides," she added as she put the stuffed peppers into the oven and slammed the door shut, "you have just as much right as anybody else to win that thousand dollars."

"But what do I have to do?" I asked, not having a clue what a Good Citizen Award might entail.

"Just get your bike and ride up to her house. Make sure you're on time." And with that, my mother sent me off to Mrs. Dayock's house to compete for the Edgewater Women's Democratic Club's Good Citizen Award.

Mrs. Dayock was clearly the fanciest lady in Edgewater. Besides being the club's president, she was also the mother of

Grace Dayock, an Edgewater girl who, unlike me, had made it onto the cheerleading squad and into the upper ranks of popularity at Leonia High School.

When I got there, Mrs. Dayock showed me into her dining room and introduced me to two other ladies, who were sipping tea from the tiniest cups I had ever seen. They held their pinkies high, and I wondered why all three ladies were wearing the same color nail polish. With their bouffant Jackie Kennedy hair and trendy outfits, they looked a lot more sophisticated than my mother. But they didn't look as nice.

Mrs. Dayock offered me the seat opposite them and began, "So, dear, what do *you* think makes a good citizen?"

"A good citizen?" I repeated, fixing my smile to hide my overbite.

"Yes, dear, a good citizen."

"Well . . ." I began, searching my head for the answer to Mrs. Dayock's riddle. "A nice person?"

"Yes," she said, nodding, and prompted, "a nice person *and* . . ."

I thought for a moment about what else might make a good citizen and added decidedly, "Just a nice person, that's all."

"Oh, that's very nice, dear," Mrs. Dayock said as she nodded toward the two other ladies, who nodded back. Mrs. Dayock stood up and gestured toward the door. "We appreciate your coming, dear." Needless to say, my pontification on good citizenry did not win me the thousand dollars.

When I got home from Chicky Dayock's, I assaulted my mother with my tale of woe. "I'm mortified, Mom, just mortified," I sputtered. "Everyone there acted like they were much better than me. And now Mrs. Dayock is going to tell Grace about my stupid answer, Grace will tell the cheerleaders, and the cheerleaders will tell the whole school! I knew I shouldn't have gone. I just knew it!"

Mom threw up her hands. "Enough," she said. "Barbara Ann, just get over yourself! Whether you won or lost isn't even important. What's important is that you had *the right to be there. Period.* Besides, taking yourself *that* seriously will only give you a heart attack."

Susan crossed her legs and shifted in her chair impatiently. Then it hit me. Susan Cara was simply a rougher version of me. She was hungry, passionate, and desperately trying to fill in the blanks.

"Okay, Susan," I said. "Since your customer is for real, and since you need help in getting access to commercial property owners, let me suggest you talk to Carrie Chiang."

"Who's she?" she snapped.

"Carrie Chiang is the number one broker in this firm," I said, "as well as the number one broker in all of Manhattan. She can get you your appointment with Mr. Trump and with any other commercial developers you need access to. Commercial developers won't give you the time of day, Susan, but they'll give it to

Carrie. I'd be happy to walk you over to her desk and introduce you right now, if you like."

I knew a woman like her would find the immediacy of my offer appealing, and she followed me through the sales area over to Carrie's section. Every salesperson turned, their eyes following her red plaid Chanel suit as her hips swayed side to side in the unmistakable age-old message that screamed, "Come and get it!"

Carrie's office was a frenzy of activity. Like a taxi dispatcher, she was working three phones at once while two assistants shuffled files. We watched and waited for a break. When Carrie finally looked up she said, "Hi, Baa-bwa, what you got?"

"Susan," I answered, "and she wants to meet with Donald Trump. Susan has a big investor from Hong Kong that is interested in the Plaza Hotel."

"Who your investor?" Carrie asked point-blank.

"Polylinks Corporation," Susan answered.

"Daniel Yiu or Jefferson Wu?" Carrie shot back.

Susan was startled. "Both," she answered slowly, squinting her eyes and trying to size up Carrie.

Carrie pushed a chair at Susan and commanded, "Sit down!"

That's how the partnership began. Susan Cara, from Queens, representing Polylinks Corporation from Hong Kong, and Carrie

Chiang, from Hong Kong, representing Donald Trump from New York. And both salespeople representing The Corcoran Group.

January 1994. The Plaza Hotel.

Susan, Carrie, and I stood outside the Plaza Hotel waiting for the Donald to appear. I was six months pregnant and feeling a little too bloated to be standing in high heels hustling a deal. A swarm of Plaza employees buzzed about on high alert, making all the necessary preparations. In the midst of all the pomp and circumstance, I felt a bit like a pauper about to witness the King's arrival at the palace gates.

At exactly eight thirty A.M., the Donald's black limousine arrived at the red-carpeted Plaza steps. A full squad of uniformed doormen opened the Plaza's brass-plated doors, tripping over themselves to say hello to Mr. Trump. "Good morning, Mr. Trump! Good morning, Mr. Trump! Mr. Trump! Good morning, sir!" they all chorused.

"Dahnul!" Carrie shouted down, her face flushed with all the excitement. "Hello, Dahnul!" She reached for Donald's hand and pointed to me. "You know Baa-bwa. And this is Susan."

"Good morning, Carrie, Susan," the Donald clipped, giving Susan the once-over. "Barbara," he said, hardly looking my way. Without another word, Donald strutted into the Plaza with his entourage, including us, in tow.

We were seated at the Donald's corner table in the Edwardian Room, overlooking Central Park South and Fifth Avenue. Donald, his financial guy, and the three of us all awaited Susan's clients. A dozen waiters fluttered around Donald, attending to his every whim.

Carrie pulled out her files and slammed them on the table. "I go over all your numbers, Dahnul," she said directly, "and I don't see numbers on the bank. Where your bank numbers, Dahnul?"

Donald Trump knew Carrie well. She had single-handedly sold fifty-three condos in Mr. Trump's financially troubled condominium on 69th Street in less than a year. She had sold them two at a time, despite the fact that the condominium market had stumbled and all the other new condominium developments weren't selling at all. Donald was so appreciative he arranged a private dinner at the Plaza Hotel to honor Carrie for her heroic rescue. He presented her with a cake and fifty-three candles, each candle representing a condo she had sold. Exhilarated by all the attention, Carrie blew them out with one big breath. "In three months, Dahnul," she proclaimed, "I sell fifty-three more!" And she did.

Carrie and Donald continued discussing the numbers, Carrie waving her hands all the while to emphasize her points.

"*Psssst!*" Susan leaned into me and whispered, "Don't forget the commission agreement."

"*What* commission agreement?" I asked.

"Our commission agreement. We don't have one."

"What do you mean we don't have a commission agreement?" I huffed in disbelief. *"Why not?"*

Susan fluttered her eyelashes and let out a little-girl giggle.

"Excuse me, Donald," I interrupted. "We need to have a commission agreement."

"Don't worry about it," he answered. "We all know each other here." And he continued to talk to Carrie.

"No, Dahnul!" Carrie said, signaling "stop" with the palm of her hand. "Our commission 3 percent! Three percent, Dahnul! If Polylink buy Plaza, if Polylink buy condos, if Polylink buy other Dahnul property, *you-pay-me-3-percent*! It commercial commission, Dahnul; *commercial commission 3 percent*. A good deal, Dahnul," she said, and waited.

"Okay, okay, Carrie, no problem," he said, and looked back down at the financial papers Carrie had brought.

I reached over and pulled the paper doily from underneath the silver sugar tray. I smoothed it out, took a pen, and wrote what I remembered to be the essential elements of a legal contract. It read: "January 11, 1994. I, Donald Trump, promise to pay The Corcoran Group, and I, Barbara Corcoran, promise to accept a three percent (3%) commission for the sale of any currently owned Donald Trump properties sold to Polylinks and/or their affiliates."

I signed my name at the bottom of the doily and drew a line for Donald Trump's signature.

"Donald," I interrupted again, "just to make sure there's no misunderstanding about the commission, I wrote down exactly what we just agreed on." I handed it to him. "Could you please sign right here next to where I signed my name?" I pointed to his name.

Donald took a quick look. "Of course I will," he said and signed his name with a thick black pen and handed me the doily.

I put the doily in my purse and checked my watch; it was 8:47. Messrs. Yiu and Wu were already seventeen minutes late. "Well, Susan?" I said quietly. "Where are they?" When she answered by giggling nervously, I wanted to rip her long legs off her fabulous body.

Donald looked around the room. "Where are the Chinese?" he demanded. "Are they coming or not?"

"Excuse me, Mr. Trump," Susan apologized coyly, pushing a strand of hair away from her face. "I think they may have gone to Trump Tower by mistake. I'll go over and get them."

Ten minutes later, Susan returned with no Wu and no Yiu. She was panting from her two-block sprint and explained that her clients were nowhere to be found. By nine fifteen, Mr. Trump decided he had waited long enough, but just as he got up to leave, two Chinese men in identical dark blue suits walked into the Edwardian Room.

"Oh, Mr. Yiu! Mr. Wu!" Susan called, swaying her way over. "Come, Mr. Yiu, Mr. Wu. I'd like you to meet Mr. Trump." The

Donald stood up, his six-foot-two frame towering over the two men.

"Really nice of you guys to come in and see me," he said, offering his hand. The Asians looked pleased to meet such a New York celebrity.

"And this is Carrie Chiang," Susan continued, "Mr. Trump's broker."

Carrie Chiang stood up and spoke in rapid Mandarin Chinese.

"*Hen rong xing ren shi ni. Xi wang ni ci xing shun li.*"

"*Hen shun li, chen xiao jie,*" Mr. Yiu responded.

"*Wo zhe li lu xing hen shun li.*" Mr. Wu nodded and agreed.

Susan looked unnerved as she lost control of her customer. She escorted them away from Carrie and over to my side of the table. "And this is Barbara Corcoran, Mr. Yiu and Mr. Wu, the president of my company."

"It's a pleasure to meet you," I said, shaking their hands and smiling. Everyone took a seat.

Carrie began her lengthy presentation on the Plaza Hotel. The Chinese men listened intently, punctuating each of her points with nods and questioning her numbers as she went. Carrie talked right, left, and in between, never losing sight of where she was going. She pulled papers, pointed to charts, and worked her calculator. When it came to numbers, Carrie could find a needle in a haystack.

Donald sat quietly, looking distracted, as though he were

already involved in some other agenda. And then he made his move. "I've got a strong gut feeling that the Plaza is not the right deal for you. I keep thinking that my Riverside South project might be more what you guys are looking for. It's a really big deal, a *really* big deal! It's going to be the largest commercial and residential project to ever hit Manhattan! Fourteen city blocks right on the Hudson River! Sixteen buildings, six thousand apartments, two million square feet of commercial space, and, would you believe it, underground parking for thirty-five hundred cars! Ready to build. It took me ten years to get the city's approval on this big deal. And Philip Johnson— you know his name, the famous architect—designed the project." He hesitated. "But, you know, guys, I shouldn't be talking about it."

"Mr. Trump, thank you. But we have no interest in new development deals," Mr. Yiu said. "We buy hotels."

"Okay," Donald said, "I probably shouldn't be talking about it anyway, as we've just about signed a deal with Colony Capital. They have a bunch of Japanese investors that are pretty excited about a 300 percent return on their investment." Then he stopped. "But since you guys are only interested in hotels, I gotta tell you, the Plaza is the best hotel in New York."

The breakfast ended at ten o'clock. As Carrie promised to send the Chinese the information they needed, Susan corrected her and said, "*I'll* send that to you, Mr. Yiu and Mr. Wu, by next week at the latest."

March 4, 1994.

I was lying in the white-sheeted bed at Mount Sinai hospital when the phone rang. After six long years and eight failed in vitro attempts, I was aglow with the miracle that I had actually given birth to a healthy nine-pound, two-ounce boy.

"Baa-bwa," a loud voice squawked on the other end of the phone. "Baa-bwa, it's Carrie. I on the plane, I on the plane and I have Dahnul."

"Oh, that's good, Carrie," I said as I shifted to adjust the bandages from my C-section. Carrie and Susan were on their way to China and were calling again to badger me into getting Donald's attorney on the phone.

"Baa-bwa, you call Dahnul's lawyer now," Carrie instructed. "You get Dahnul's lawyer to send the papers now. Okay?"

"Okay, Carrie," I said. "I'm sorry I haven't gotten to it yet but I've been a little busy. Oh, and by the way, Carrie, I had a baby."

It took five and a half months, nineteen meetings, two trips to Hong Kong, twenty-seven hundred pages of faxed documents, and seventeen attorneys, but on June 30, 1994, the deal closed, and the six wealthiest families in Hong Kong became one of the largest landlords in Manhattan, purchasing the outstanding $310 million debt from the banks on fourteen city blocks along the Hudson River for the bargain price of $90 million, plus another $8 million in real estate taxes.

To no one's surprise, Carrie Chiang continued to smash her own sales records year after year. But Susan's career proved short lived. Soon after the sale, she divorced her mechanic husband and snagged herself a renowned internist, retiring to their luxurious new abode in Westchester County.

22

You've Got to Bully
a Bully

June 1994.

As it turns out, I had lost the commission doily a few days after the first breakfast at the Plaza Hotel and had been too afraid to tell Carrie and Susan. Our attorney knew, and had used it to bluff Donald into agreeing to sign a new commission agreement, threatening to sue on the basis of a doily that didn't exist.

But Donald had negotiated us down, and the final agreement stipulated that our commission would be $4 million and would be paid out in installments. Each payment was due by the tenth business day of every month and if it was late, the entire commission became immediately due.

The week before the deal closed, I picked up the phone and called *New York* magazine, the gossipy New York weekly always eager to break a sensational story. The business editor told me that they were about to run a cover story that said Donald Trump was finished. He said that although Citicorp had already renegotiated Donald's debt of $993 million, they were about to foreclose on his prestigious Plaza Hotel anyway.

"Well, what I'm about to tell you might just change your story," I said.

On the tenth business day of July, Donald's first check arrived at my office, hand-delivered by his messenger at 4:48 P.M. The messenger had been instructed to hand it only to me and to have me sign the receipt. I called Esther, Carrie, and Susan and waited for them to arrive before opening the envelope, then I asked Sylvia to immediately send Donald a large bouquet of flashy flowers from Remy's on Park Avenue. I asked that the florist include a note that read, "Thank you for your check, Donald. We so much appreciate it." And sign it Barbara, Carrie, and Susan.

When everyone arrived at our office, we drank champagne and celebrated our first installment, a check for $55,555.55.

August 1994.

I gulped when I saw the caricature of Donald Trump on the cover of *New York* magazine, precariously hanging on to the ledge of a high-rise building. I was at a newsstand on the corner of 60th and Madison as I read the bold headline:

TRUMP'S NEAR-DEATH EXPERIENCE

By the time I got to the office, Donald had already called once. When he called again, I carefully picked up the phone and said as cheerfully as I could, "Good morning, Donald."

Donald's voice barked into my ear. *"How could you let Carrie and that Susan lady speak to a reporter? Can't you keep your girls in check over there?"*

"Donald," I said, "you know I'm not in control of Carrie; you know how she is. And as for Susan, she's young and inexperienced, and you can't fault her for that. But, personally, I think today's story makes you look great! In fact, I think it makes you look like a miracle worker—" Donald Trump didn't agree with my assessment and abruptly hung up the phone.

When the next check arrived, again by messenger, I signed for it and instructed Sylvia to send an even larger bouquet of flashy flowers. Two hours later, the bouquet arrived back at my office, returned by Mr. Trump's messenger. On the unopened envelope was scribbled, "Return to sender." I got a sick feeling in my stomach that things were about to get worse.

Things got worse. The next day, the summons and complaint arrived, claiming "breach of contract." Donald was suing *us* to cancel the $4 million commission (not yet paid) and to recover damages.

SUPREME COURT OF THE STATE OF NEW YORK
COUNTY OF NEW YORK
- - - - - - - - - - - - - - - - X
DONALD TRUMP,

                           Plaintiff,

-against-

THE CORCORAN GROUP, INC.,
BARBARA CORCORAN, CARRIE CHIANG
and SUSAN CARA,

                          Defendants.
—————————————————— X

                    60 Centre Street
                    New York, New York
                    May 20, 1996

           BEFORE: HONORABLE IRA
           GAMMERMAN, JUSTICE

"Let's get a big guy!" Carrie said. "Dahnul not fair! We need a *big* lawyer." Susan agreed with Carrie, but Esther had already met with our regular attorney, and after reviewing the papers, he said he was confident he could win the case. Although I wanted to believe in his confidence, something gnawed at me after everyone left my office.

I opened my drawer, took out the *New York* magazine article, and found the passage that was echoing in my brain. Donald was quoted as saying, "You learn that either you're the toughest, meanest piece of shit in the world or you just crawl into a corner, put your finger in your mouth, and say, 'I want to go home.'"

A chill ran up my spine.

After school. The kitchen table.

My brother Tommy was so upset he couldn't tell my mother what was wrong. "Well, you can't stay in here all day," Mom said. "You should be outside playing with the other boys."

"I don't *want* to," Tommy cried. "I don't want to go outside and see that kid again!"

"And what kid is that?" Mom asked, wiping Tommy's face with a cold washcloth.

"J-Joey B-Bunt," Tommy said. "He says really mean things to me, Mom, and he embarrasses me in front of all the other boys."

John boosted himself up onto the counter and reached for the pinwheels that Mom kept hidden above the stove. "Isn't that the same kid who puts cherry bombs in cats?" John asked.

"He does what?" Mom asked.

"Yeah, that's him, that's the same mean kid," Tommy sniffled. "And that's not all! He's a big bully! I saw him kick Mrs. Gibbons's dog—you know, the little scrawny one with the brown spots."

"Well, Tommy," Mom said, "sooner or later you're going to have to face him, because he's probably not planning to move out of Edgewater."

"Yeah, and I'll go with you, Tom," John offered confidently.

"Well, if he's a bully," Mom said, "you're going to need more than two nice boys to handle him. Let me call Mrs. Higgins and ask if Brendan can go with you."

"We don't need Brendan to come with us, Mom," John said. "I'm big enough."

"Oh, no, you're not," Mom insisted. "You've got to bully a bully, and Brendan can do that easier because he's bigger."

That day, Brendan Higgins whipped Joey Bunt's butt and Joey never bothered my brother Tommy again.

I picked up the phone and called Carrie. "Carrie," I said, "you're right. We need to find ourselves a great litigator to fight Mr. Trump."

1996. Supreme Court of the State of New York.

The moment Richard Seltzer walked into the courtroom, I knew
we weren't going to be pushed around. Richard was just the
right guy, tough enough and smart enough to bully a bully. I had
to remind myself that the ball of fire burning up the courtroom
was the same quiet attorney who had spent hours meticulously
reviewing every possible question that we might be asked.

Donald Trump's claim was that, as his agent, we had breached
our fiduciary responsibility by disclosing confidential information
in the *New York* magazine article. Our defense was that everything Carrie and Susan said in the article was *not* confidential,
because Donald had already bragged the same details to dozens of other reporters before the *New York* magazine story ever
came out.

Donald looked startled when Richard Seltzer pulled out his
stack of four-color, five-foot charts with blown-up quotes of
what Donald had said, when, and to whom. He had prepared
separate boards quoting Donald spilling the beans to the *Wall
Street Journal* on June 8, to the *South China Morning Post* on
June 10, to the *New York Observer* on June 13, and to *Crain's
New York Business* on June 20. "Are these not your quotes, Mr.
Trump?" Richard demanded in a booming voice as he cross-
examined the Donald on the stand.

———

In rendering his decision, Judge Ira Gammerman said, "Of all the witnesses, my view is that Miss Corcoran's recollection is the most reliable. I tell you that. . . . And I find as a matter of fact that there was no fraudulent inducement. We have a *bruised ego*, is what this case is all about. And I'm telling you, I find, as a matter of fact, that those are the only damages in this case."

We won the lawsuit and were entitled to the rest of our $4 million commission.

23

Never Be Ashamed
of Who You Are

December 1997.

"Howard Milstein on the phone," Sylvia announced.

I had never met Mr. Howard Milstein, but rumor had it that the New York billionaire had paid only $12 million to buy my competitor six years earlier. He had bought Douglas Elliman Real Estate at the depth of the real estate recession from a group of investors who had milked the company dry. Twelve million dollars sounded like a ton of money to me, but people in the finance field called it a bargain-basement price.

Under Mr. Milstein's leadership, Douglas Elliman combined

the one-two punch of old-money prestige and good-old-boy power. Although his company had a larger market share than we did, The Corcoran Group was gaining fast, and I suspected that Mr. Milstein didn't like that very much.

"Hi, it's Barbara," I chirped as I picked up the phone, wondering why my archrival was calling me.

"Hold for Mr. Milstein," his secretary said, and put me on hold in what I find to be one of the most annoying practices of people in power.

"Good morning, Barbara," a clipped but polite voice said on the other end of the phone. "I'd like to get together and discuss some business."

"Some business?" I asked. "What kind of business?"

"*Our* business," he said. "Let's discuss it over a cocktail, shall we? How about tomorrow?"

"I can't," I said with relief. "I'm leaving with my family for a vacation in Australia tomorrow and will be gone for two weeks."

"Fine, then let's say two weeks from tomorrow," he replied. "That will be the twenty-fourth. We'll meet at my home. Shall we say four P.M.?"

Before I could say "jet lag," I had agreed to the date.

The twenty-four hours back from Australia seemed a lot longer than the twenty-four hours getting there, and when I landed at

JFK airport, I had exactly eighty minutes to find my luggage, hop a cab to Manhattan, change clothes, and present myself at Mr. Milstein's home on Park Avenue.

I got home, dropped my luggage, threw on a suit, and headed out. I stopped at a Korean fruit stand on Lexington Avenue and quickly paid for a bunch of daisies. "No need to wrap," I said, and rushed over to Park Avenue and 78th Street. When I arrived at Mr. Milstein's building, a uniformed doorman with lots of gold braiding announced my arrival.

"Miss Corcoran for Mr. Milstein," he said into the front-door phone. He motioned me toward another man in gold braid, who ushered me into a brass-gated elevator. When the elevator doors opened, I didn't have to guess which door was Mr. Milstein's. There was only one. The door was made of gleaming mahogany, and standing at attention holding it open was a man in a long-tailed coat. He looked as if he were dressed for a wedding.

"Goooood afternooooon!" he said, finishing his o's and bowing his head as if to collect a thought he'd lost. "Mr. Milstein is expecting you, m'daahm. Please follow me."

He turned on his heel like a palace guard, and feeling rather awkward, I followed behind. The huge entrance gallery was bigger than our house in Edgewater and it had some serious museum-type paintings hanging on the walls. There were lots of tables decorated with the largest flower arrangements I'd ever seen. "Please wait here, m'daahm," he instructed as we got to the middle of the runway. "I'll tell Mr. Milstein you've arrived." I tucked my Korean deli daisies behind my back and was thinking about stashing them under one of the big tables when Mr. Milstein suddenly appeared.

"So nice of you to come, Barbara!" he welcomed, while eagerly shaking my hand. "Perhaps we'll sit in the den, James," he said. James nodded, turned on his heel, and walked back in the direction we had just come. I followed along again, with Mr. Milstein bringing up the rear.

Mr. Milstein looked surprised to find Mrs. Milstein sitting in the den. He politely introduced me, and she politely helloed me back, and I decided it was as good a time as any to unload my three-dollar daisies.

I pulled the daisies from behind my back and felt like Timmy Tom when he handed my mother the gladiolus he'd yanked from our yard. "These are for you, Mrs. Milstein," I said. Mrs. Milstein hesitated, and then took them, ignoring the rubber band at the bottom. "Why, thank you," she said softly. "How sweet."

"You're welcome," I said, smiling, but somehow felt I had done something wrong.

"Let us try the library, then, shall we?" Mr. Milstein pleasantly decided, and again we trotted off into the gallery, led by James. "Good-bye," I quickly said to Mrs. Milstein and the daisies.

The trip down the Milstein runway was beginning to feel like the flight back from Australia, and when we finally arrived at the library, James ceremoniously opened the heavy paneled doors to a huge room filled with books, chairs, and tables with lamps all around. James stepped to the side, folding his arms behind his back.

"What will you have to drink, Barbara?" Mr. Milstein asked as he motioned to a brown leather club chair.

"White wine, please," I said, settling in.

"And what kind would you prefer?" he asked with a tight smile.

"White, thank you," I replied.

James walked out, quietly closing the doors behind him. I sat straight in my chair, smiling, and trying to figure out why I was there.

"The Corcoran Group seems to be progressing quite nicely," Mr. Milstein offered.

"Why, thank you, Mr. Milstein," I said, scanning the plaques, trophies, and diplomas that surrounded us. "It's very nice of you to say that, Mr. Milstein, and I really appreciate hearing it."

"Barbara, please call me Howard."

"Okay, then, Howard, please call me Barbara."

I decided to keep quiet for a while because I didn't know what to talk about, and although Mr. Milstein—I mean, Howard—was talking to me as though I was his new best friend, I kept thinking of him as my competitor, and didn't think those two things usually came together. James walked back in, handed each of us our drink, set down some small plates and napkins, and left.

"I really do admire how far you've come with your company, Barbara," Mr. Milstein continued. "You strike me as a very smart businesswoman."

"Thank you, Howard," I said, feeling more uncomfortable than smart. "But I'm really not smart at all; I just work really hard." I took a chug of my wine.

"Well, I'm sure you're smart enough to recognize a good business idea when you hear one. I think we could have great synergism if we were to work together."

"Sinner-jizzum," I repeated slowly. "I'm embarrassed to admit that I don't know what that word means." I realized I was way out of my league, and probably shouldn't have come.

Mr. Milstein closed his hands with his forefingers raised in a V, leaned way back in his chair, and expounded, "Well, Barbara, then let me take a moment to explain it to you. Synergism is a business term I learned at Harvard. It simply means joining two strong companies to create a stronger one that's able to do more business. It's really quite simple, like one plus one equals three."

"I think I get it," I said. "Yes, one plus one equals three! You're really a wonderful teacher and you obviously know a lot about business, Mr. Milstein! Now, what two companies were you thinking about putting together?"

"What? Well, mine and yours, of course!"

The mahogany doors opened and James wheeled in a large silver cart. He lifted a tray, genuflected in front of me, and said, "Ooorrr durrrrve?"

I looked down at the food in front of me. I was ferociously hungry and beginning to feel the jet lag and wine settling in. The food on the tray didn't look like anything I'd seen before. It looked a little bit like mini-burritos, but not exactly, because it had pink stuff inside. There were also little black things on top that looked like chocolate sprinkles. But I leaned in for a closer look, and though I had never tried caviar before, I realized by its wetness that that's probably what it was.

"M'daahm?" James offered, waiting in his bent position.

I decided to go for it because I thought it would be rude not to, and I was also really hungry. "Oh, thank you," I said.

Using my hand like the metal claw in the Palisades Amusement Park crane game, I reached down for the "burrito." I tried to get a good hold on it, but it was wetter than I thought and both the pink stuff and the caviar sprinkles kept sliding around. Finally, I grabbed it and popped the sucker into my mouth. The burrito filled every bit of my mouth, and I could hardly chew.

"Will that be . . . all, m'daahm?" James asked without moving, his eyes wide, as if he were giving me a signal to take more.

I shook my head no and answered, "Hwumm hwmum," which was my stuffed-mouth version of "Thank you, James, that will be all."

James moved over to Mr. Milstein and offered him the tray.

Mr. Milstein took a small silver fork and knife and a little plate from the table between us. He lifted a burrito and gracefully placed it on his plate. As I continued trying to chew, Mr. Milstein cut off a small piece, nudged it onto his fork, and tipped it into his mouth. He nodded at James and said, "Mmmm, perfect!"

Oh, God, I thought, gumming at my mouthful of mush, *so that's what the little knife and fork are for!*

Girl Scouts. The Fort Lee Pizzeria.

The first time I ever had pizza was with Miss Griffin and seven Girl Scouts. Miss Griffin, our eighth-grade teacher, was the only Holy Rosary School teacher who wasn't a nun. She had taken us to see *To Kill a Mockingbird* at the Fort Lee Movie Theater, and afterward, we went to the Fort Lee Pizzeria to have pizza.

When our pizza came, we all lifted a slice onto our paper plates and waited for it to cool. I followed Grace Dayock's lead on how to eat it. Grace raised the pizza to her mouth and chomped down. I raised my pizza to my mouth and chomped down, too. But my teeth couldn't cut the cheese. My overbite wouldn't allow it.

I kept the pizza against my lips and looked around the table. The other Girl Scouts were well into their slices and hadn't noticed the pizza still stuck in my mouth. I grated my teeth back and forth, but the cheese just shifted along with my teeth. I opened my mouth to let go of the pizza, folded the dented tip back onto the slice, and quietly put the pizza back on my plate.

When I got home, Mom had just finished her bath. "What's for dinner, Mom?" I said through the bathroom door.

"Nothing," she answered. "Dinner was at six. Didn't you eat dinner with the Girl Scouts and Miss Griffin?"

"Nope."

"Well, why not?" Mom asked, as she came out of the bathroom.

"My overbite wouldn't let me eat the pizza."

"That's pretty funny," she laughed. "So, why didn't you ask for a plate of spaghetti or something? Or just a knife and fork?"

"I couldn't," I said. "I was too embarrassed."

"Embarrassed? Why would you be embarrassed?"

"I didn't want anyone to see my buckteeth."

"Ha! That's ridiculous!" Mom huffed. "I'm sure the Girl Scouts have seen your buckteeth before. Besides, Barbara Ann, you have a beautiful smile, and you should never be ashamed of who you are. Now, why don't you go over to the refrigerator and find yourself something to eat?"

Mr. Milstein spoke slowly. "Let me explain to you some of the synergisms we might enjoy together," he said. "Take advertising, for example. We would have a lot more buying clout and be able to negotiate substantial discounts if we were together."

"Hmmmm," I answered, my eyes watering as I swallowed the tail end of the fishy mush.

"And we could cut the expenses of our back-office operations in half," he suggested, "possibly in thirds. We could also combine our individual offices and keep only the best salespeople. I'm sure you're carrying a lot of deadwood, like we are, and together we could eliminate it.

"And you could run both businesses!" he enthused. "And you'd be in charge of many more people than you are now."

James came back in and lowered his tray to offer me another burrito. "M'daahm?" he asked again. I stared down at the tray of food I didn't want, but not wanting to offend my host, and not wanting to offend James for offering it, I decided I'd better take another.

I looked at the little knife and fork on the table next to my chair. With them I could eat as delicately as Mr. Milstein. But thinking about my mother, I decided I didn't want to.

"Oh, thank you," I said.

I lifted my hand and craned it over a burrito. Grabbing it dead center, I popped it into my mouth. "Mmmm." I smiled.

Mr. Milstein talked on and on about synergies, market shares, diminishing returns, and a lot of other things that I wasn't educated enough to know about, had always heard about, and didn't really care about. Then he began his grand finale.

"Barbara, together our companies would have the majority control of the Manhattan real estate market," he said. "And our combined companies could be sold for a lot more money than if we sold them separately."

I looked at Mr. Milstein and tried to picture him as my partner. Or would he be my employer? I wasn't sure. Maybe he just wanted to buy me wholesale and sell me retail. I didn't know.

"Well then, what do you think?" he asked confidently as he inched toward me in his leather chair.

"Would you like a political answer or an honest one?" I asked.

"An honest answer, of course," he said.

"No," I said. And with that, I thanked Mr. Milstein for the delicious food and the wonderful education and bade him good-bye.

Mr. Milstein's offer turned out to be the first in a long line of similar propositions. But none of my suitors ever asked what my dreams and aspirations were *before* they started their sales pitch. If they had, they would have discovered that my personal goals had nothing to do with money, status, or power.

But my visit with Mr. Milstein got me thinking, and for the first time, I realized I had a business actually worth something! I decided to size up where I had been, where I was now, and, most important, where I wanted to go.

I realized that my dream of being the Queen of New York Real Estate had come true. I had taken the company from Ray Simone's $1,000 investment and the 1 BR + DEN ad to what was about to become the number one firm in the New York market. I had climbed my mountain and achieved everything I had set out to do, and had proven to myself that I could succeed without him.

Thanks to the fabulous market of the nineties, The Corcoran Group was hugely profitable and had ended the year with more than $2 billion in sales. Our salespeople and employees were known as the best in the business. We had twelve beautifully designed offices equipped with the most advanced technology, and it was *all* paid for. In short, The Corcoran Group was in mint condition.

But I had seen bad times, too, and considered myself lucky to have made it through. With our overhead now more than a million dollars a month, liquidating my personal assets wouldn't be enough to carry the business through another downturn. I knew we needed deeper pockets.

I thought about taking on a financial partner as a minority shareholder, but knew that in bad times the partner with the most money often wrestles away majority control. I realized I was much too independent for that.

What I treasured most about building the business was working with all our great people and running the company hand in hand like a family. But now there were so many people at the company, I no longer knew each person's name, and that bothered me.

Most important, I was now the mother of a little boy, and my heart was torn between my family at home and my family at work. I felt guilty when I wasn't with my son and guilty when I wasn't with my business. My pursuit of the elusive balance that every working mom chases was proving impossible.

I came to the realization that my business was all grown up, and ready to leave Mom and go out on its own. I soon found someone who not only offered me the right price but also offered me enough freedom and enough latitude to continue making The Corcoran Group the best in the business.

Besides, I had been "Barbara Corcoran, the real estate lady" for so long, I started thinking it might be nice to see what it was like to be just Barbara Corcoran.

24

The Joy Is in the Getting There

September 2001.

As we turned the corner onto Madison Avenue, I was cherishing the fact that my seven-year-old son was still willing to walk beside me and hold my hand. But, as usual, he dropped it at the first sighting of the bigger boys standing in front of his school and gave me his quick-while-nobody's-looking sideways hug and darted inside. As the door closed behind him, I thought, *My God, how fast it's going*, and mourned the end of another day walking my little boy to school.

I stopped by our new real estate office, on the corner of Madison Avenue, and picked up the packet of newspaper clippings my assistant had left for me to read. I tucked the envelope under my arm, crossed over to the Korean deli, and picked out my weekly bunch of six-dollar flowers. As I got to the cashier, I remembered I didn't have any cash. I apologized, put the flowers back, and made a beeline to the ATM at the Citibank across the street.

All the machines were taken, and I stood in line behind a woman whose gray and white hair was styled just like her Yorkie's. When it was my turn, I stepped up to the machine on the far left side, put in my bank card, entered my security code, tapped "Fast Cash," then "$200." I heard the familiar tat-a-tat-a-tat, tat-a-tat-a-tat, as the machine counted out the money, and was relieved to hear the *errrrrrk* as the stack of twenties slid out the front. I put the cash in my Filofax and took the receipt.

On my way to the garbage can by the front window, I took a quick look at the receipt before tossing it in. My arm screeched to a halt. I stared at the receipt in utter disbelief and moved it closer, squinting my eyes to make sure I wasn't imagining things. I turned my head left and then right like an owl, looking to see if anyone was watching. No one was. The Yorkie lady passed me and smiled. Moving closer to the window, I tilted the receipt toward the light to take another look.

Date	Time	Location	Card Number
Sep 25, 2001	8:37	000062	Ending in 036
1275 Madison, NY, NY			

Transaction	Amount	Description
GOT CASH	$200.00	FROM CHECKING

BALANCES

On deposit	$46,732,917.32	CHECKING
Available now	$46,732,917.32	

citibank®

Yes, the balance really did read $46,732,917.32! I was absolutely sure of it. *My God*, I thought, *I've got to show this to someone!* The six people standing at the teller machines had their backs to me, and suddenly the thought of showing any of them my receipt seemed ridiculous. But I just couldn't go home. I needed to do *something* to celebrate.

I carefully folded the blue and white receipt in half, tucked it into my bra, and walked over to the diner next door. I picked a seat at the empty table by the window and quickly straightened out the sugar container, ketchup bottle, and salt and pepper shakers before the waitress came over.

"What can I get you, honey?" she asked.

What the heck, I thought, *I'll go whole hog today. After all, this isn't just any old day!* "I'll have eggs Benedict, a large glass of orange juice, and coffee, please," I said. The waitress was wearing a rhinestone heart pinned to her white collar, and I added, "That's really a lovely pin you have there."

"Oh, thank you," she said, seeming grateful that I had noticed. "It was my mother's."

When my eggs arrived, I took out the Citibank receipt from my bra, smoothed out the crease, and leaned it against the sugar dispenser. I took a sip of hot coffee and wondered if Esther had visited *her* bank yet. I laughed at the thought of Esther quickly tucking her bank receipt into her pocketbook and snapping it shut. I remembered the chart I'd drawn the day I talked Esther into becoming my partner, and the wild projections of how far we would go. Things had turned out even bigger than we had dared to imagine.

I thought about all the incredible adventures we had had building the business, and how lucky I was to have been given the freedom to create a world just as I dreamt it could be. I thought about the people who had stood by me through thick and thin, and how everyone at The Corcoran Group had built great lives for themselves. And I felt the immense satisfaction of a job well done.

The boring man at the next table was telling his sister all the news she had missed while she was away on a trip of some kind. He yakked on and on about the bad economy, Republican politics, and the city's terrible school system. When they were finished, the man paid the bill, turned to his sister, and said,

"Oh, and did you hear Barbara Corcoran sold her business for mega-millions?" He didn't wait for a response before adding, "Must be nice to have all that money in the bank."

Yes, I guess it is, I reflected, *but the real joy has been in getting here.*

I opened the packet of newspaper articles and read through the pile of clippings.

The New York Times

TUESDAY, SEPTEMBER 25, 2001

Corcoran Sells Realty Firm She Founded

Cashing Out After Years Of Rising Housing Prices

By ANDREW ROSS SORKIN

Barbara Corcoran, the powerhouse Manhattan real estate broker, agreed yesterday to sell the firm she founded, The Corcoran Group.

NEW YORK POST
LATE CITY FINAL
September 25, 2001

It's official: Corcoran to Cendant

By BRADEN KEIL

Following an emotionally charged company meeting last Friday, Barbara Corcoran sent a memo to company employees announcing the sale of The Corcoran Group.

....

CRAIN'S
NEW YORK BUSINESS®
October 1–7, 2001

Corcoran's home run

... Although terms of the transaction weren't disclosed, people close to the deal say it was priced at $70 million.

OUR TOWN

Queen of NY Real Estate

If you're looking for new digs in New York, and dwell in one of the loftier tax brackets, chances are you've heard of Barbara Corcoran. Even if you're having trouble making the rent on that studio in Astoria, you know her face. She's the short-haired blonde sporting an incandescent smile in that commercial with the catchy song and fabulous apartments. In her 28 years as head of The Corcoran Group, she has reached the pinnacle of the toughest real estate market this side of Tokyo.

....

WOMEN'S BUSINESS
October 2001

After Merger, Corcoran Group Remains Fully Intact

. . . and that equates to a tremendous increase in business since 1973, when Corcoran began selling real estate from her Manhattan apartment on a $1,000-loan from her former boyfriend. He footed the cash for her new venture on the condition that he would own a controlling interest.

Eventually, Corcoran dissolved the partnership. From that moment on, she was bound and determined to make it in the real estate business on her own. By all accounts, she has achieved her goal.

> Corcoran has been dubbed the "most sought after broker in the city," according to CNN, and is known as the broker to Hollywood celebrities and wealthy individuals.
>
> *Exactly how did the Edgewater, NJ native become one of the most powerful figures in New York City real estate?*

"Exactly how?" I repeated the article's question. "My mother," I answered.

I slid a twenty under the saucer and headed back to my apartment. I had an important call to make.

"Hello, Mom. It's Barb. Can you get Dad on the line?"

"Eddie, pick up the phone! It's Barb."

"Hi, Mom. Hi, Dad. You'll never believe what happened at the bank today," I began. Then I told my parents about waiting in line for the teller machine to get my usual $200 cash, and how I couldn't believe my eyes when I looked down at the receipt. "I'm telling you, Mom, I just couldn't believe it! I thought I was seeing things!"

"Well, what did you do?" Mom asked excitedly.

"I did just what you would have done. I went and had some breakfast and sat there staring at the receipt."

"What'd you eat?" Dad asked.

"Eat? Oh, eggs Benedict."

"Eggs what?"

"Never mind, Eddie," Mom interrupted. "Go on! Go on!"

"So, I sat at the diner, and I thought about how it's true what you've always said, Mom; the joy really is in the getting there."

"Well, that's because it is," she agreed. "But just think about what you've done, Barbara! It really is unbelievable, isn't it?

"Yeah, I guess it really is."

And then I said what I'd wanted to say for a very long time. "In the end, Mom, it all comes down to this: All my life, you never told me I couldn't. You only told me I could."

PART TWO

Swimming with the Sharks

Seven Years Later . . .

I was on a plane to Los Angeles, my heart ka-thumping with excitement, feeling like a giddy, starstruck kid. *This is it,* I thought. *The big kahuna, everything I've been waiting for!* I was on my way to Hollywood and a whole new adventure, feeling like real happiness might finally be within my grasp. I could barely sit still in my seat.

The past seven years had been the most challenging of my life. After selling my company for $66 million, I knew I had to be absolutely crazy not to feel on top of the world, but instead, I just felt sad. I hadn't expected to feel such an incredible sense of loss and it hit me like a giant punch in the gut. Everyone I knew thought I had it all, but I was secretly miserable.

Right after NRT took control of The Corcoran Group, I felt my entire identity gone—wiped out. Getting up in the morning I stared at my closet not knowing what clothes I should wear, sometimes changing five times before walking out the door. In title, I remained the chairman of The Corcoran Group for two long years, but honestly I felt like an impostor. I had allowed the new president to take over the high-profile functions I used to do, like talking to reporters, giving speeches, and leading our salespeople, and I missed it all terribly. I even missed picking the look and feel of the company's advertising right down to the font size and paper stock. Without any decision-making power, I was just occupying space.

I had already achieved what most people would have called the American Dream. I was the amazing rags-to-riches story and had taken the thousand dollars Ray had loaned me and turned it into a billion-dollar business. I had realized my dream of becoming the undisputed Queen of New York Real Estate and, sure, I was getting to spend more time with my family, but I had no real purpose at the company and felt like a nobody.

I wasn't at all comfortable being a multimillionaire, quickly discovering that money wasn't all it was cracked up to be. I had always been good at making money, but I didn't know a damn thing about keeping it. I actually missed *worrying* about money and all the creative things I dreamt up and did to get it. People often think money can solve all their problems, but I found that having money brought a whole new set of problems.

I had always felt more at home with cabdrivers and doormen than with fancy people, but quickly learned that when you have a ton of money it's the fancy people who want to know you. Even my closest friends treated me differently. They had grown comfortable through the years with my notoriety, but having a friend with *so much* money seemed like an uncomfortable fit. Maybe it was just me, but rather than taking kindnesses as genuine, I found myself second-guessing motives. I felt guarded, fearing that people liked me only for my money. It seemed everybody I knew had a thousand-dollar problem, and I happily doled out the cash that meant so little to me and seemingly so much to them.

Not seeing my face anymore in the company's full-page ads and on billboards was bad enough, but one day I walked into the office, past the glass refrigerated units with the newly instituted beverage limit, and there in the hallway was a familiar face sticking out of the trash bin—*mine*. Someone had thrown away the poster of my smiling face that had always hung in the reception area. It felt exactly like the day I got replaced by Ray Simòne's new girlfriend Tina. That was the moment I realized I had been wrong to hang around The Corcoran Group as excess baggage for two years too many. *Okay, I get it*, I thought. *I'm outta here.*

I rented a gorgeous white horse for my good-bye party and dressed in a shiny white cowgirl outfit. I waved good-bye to my thousand brokers and rode my horse out the door, expecting to ride off into the sunset and live happily ever after. What I didn't know was that I was about to face the toughest time of my life.

I spent the next year writing a juicy memoir about the unconventional lessons I had learned from my mother and how they had helped me build my business. (Sound familiar?) It made the best-seller list and, more important, gave my mom the credit she was well overdue. I bought my mom and dad a beachfront penthouse with a La-Z-Boy chair for my dad to watch his new big-screen TV and enough room for their twenty-six grandchildren to visit.

But I was running around with a deep sadness and didn't know how to fix it. I should have probably seen a shrink, but had gotten in the habit of solving my own problems. Desperate to find a new way to define myself, I reeled from one scheme to the next. A school for dyslexics? Renovating apartments to flip? Opening a public relations company? But I just couldn't muster enough passion to get anything off the ground. I felt sure I had lost my touch and concluded that my success with The Corcoran Group had just been a fluke.

I hated my own insecurity, the negative self-talk, and the quiet doubts. I hated catching myself thinking and living in past tense: "when I used to do this . . ." or "when I used to do that . . ." When I'd run into people I knew on the streets who eagerly asked, "So, what are you up to?" I didn't have a good answer. I felt like falling to my knees and confessing my utter failure: "I'm up to nothing, absolutely nothing."

I missed the power of my old position and the constant attention that came along with it. But what I missed most of all was the day-to-day operations of being mother to a thousand adoring brokers, and all the parties and the fun I had planning for them. When the company that bought my company made the decision to block all e-mails between my old colleagues and me, I was devastated.

My whole life I'd been okay with looking brave on the outside when I was scared to death on the inside, but I wasn't okay with it anymore. I came to the conclusion that I'd better sit down and size up the changes I'd have to make to get to the next chapter of my life.

I set out to totally reinvent myself, but knew I couldn't change my wiring and decided I'd have to repackage myself instead. I pulled out my yellow legal pad and did what had always worked for me before. I drew a line down the center of the page and started making a list of everything I hated on one side and everything I loved on the other. I hated sitting at home with no place to go. I hated not having anything exciting to talk about over dinner when it came to what happened and didn't happen in my day. I hated not having one big dream of who I wanted to be. What I loved hadn't changed at all. I loved creating ideas, loved helping other people, and loved getting attention.

I decided I'd need to reinvent myself in stages. Even if I figured out exactly who I wanted to be, I was going to have to settle for achieving it a little at a time. I made up my mind to focus on getting one paid gig in the media world and to use it as a confirmation that I was on the right road. And if I could use it to boost my confidence, I just might start crawling my way to a home run. So I decided to let go of getting it right and settle for getting it going.

My old contacts proved useless when I called. They were polite and respectful, but at the end of the conversation I couldn't help feeling like old news. I had to wrap my head around the fact that I was starting from scratch again, despite everything I had done before. And if I was going to be successful, I was going to have to put in hard hours and a 150 percent effort. Although I had always hoped to find a better balance between work and play, I came to the conclusion that for me, there was no such thing as part time.

I pitched a real estate advice column for the *Daily News* and was thankful to get it, but hated the weekly deadline for the next two years. I wrote a monthly column for *Redbook* magazine giving business advice and was assigned an editor adept at editing out all of my personality. Because I wrote the real estate column, Fox News Channel called wanting to interview me about some pending real estate legislation. And that was my first lucky break.

I prepared for the next day's interview so hard that I could have written the new legislation myself. A month later, Fox offered me a regular spot as a political commentator. I laughed out loud. I had never read a newspaper in my life and didn't even know which Bush was in office. What a joke! But I jumped at the offer. I stayed up nights memorizing important people's names and read a fifth-grade primer on how the U.S. government works and even knew the difference between the House and the Senate. I felt ridiculous faking a personality, but it was the only job I could get.

I realized if I could hold my own talking about things I knew nothing about, that if I could work my way into talking about something I really knew, like business and real estate, I might be good as a TV personality. So I set my sights on the TV world, swallowed my anxiety, and started knocking on doors.

I began calling every television network head I could think of, and to my relief people recognized my name and returned my calls. They even agreed to meetings. Each one went the same way: The TV honcho would sit in his big office and listen to my spiel, nod approvingly, and say, "Sounds interesting. Let me talk to my team." Then he'd ask me for my personal advice on real estate, and once I gave it, I'd never hear from him again.

The more successful you've been, the greater the insult

when someone doesn't bother to return your call. I hated people not calling me back. I remembered that when I was head of The Corcoran Group, *everyone* called me back because I was in a position to do something for them. I decided to get over myself and keep calling.

My trial-by-fire stint at Fox helped me get the exposure that led to a call from a producer at *Good Morning America* who was looking for an expert to address the real estate bubble, which was getting ready to burst. I went on air, giving advice to homeowners wanting to sell their homes. It was something I knew a lot about. Then, armed with a pitch reel of my few TV appearances and a list of four hundred real estate story ideas, I ran over to the *Today* show and got the job as their weekly real estate contributor. With their eight million viewers each morning, I landed right where I wanted to be.

Two years later, a call came in from Mark Burnett Productions, the famous creator of *Survivor* and *The Apprentice*. I couldn't believe it. They were working on a high-stakes reality show called *Shark Tank*, which they were about to produce for Sony and ABC. The show's pitch was simple: Five tough business titans meet with aspiring entrepreneurs to consider investing in their startup companies. The catch was it was *my own cash* I'd be investing. Would I care to audition to be one of the Sharks?

I knew immediately this was the one for me, the real lucky break I'd been dreaming about! It was a perfect fit. "Of course I'd be interested," I said. And three weeks later, I signed the *Shark Tank* contract.

I pictured my new life in Hollywood in living color and marched myself right over to Bergdorf Goodman to get ready. I felt like I was about to step into somebody else's dream. I bought my new Hollywood ensemble, not only the one black outfit requested by the show, but six more. I didn't even like black and never wore it, but I wanted to look the part of the slick shark I would soon become. I also picked out three new outfits to wear before the show, four new outfits for after the show, and two extra ones just for signing autographs. I added three pairs of expensive sunglasses, two pairs of Jimmy Choos, and a pair of black Armani boots to my pile, covered my eyes, and signed the charge.

Two weeks before I was to board the flight to Hollywood, Mark Burnett's assistant was on the line. "I have some disappointing news," she said. "We've decided to hire someone else as our female shark and won't be needing you in L.A." I couldn't believe it and asked her to repeat it, and when she did, I replied, "*Who is she?*"

I Googled my competitor and found exactly what I expected—a thirtysomething blond bombshell. I clunked my sixty-year-old head down onto my desk and all my insecurities, doubts, and uncertainties overwhelmed me. Two minutes later, I collected myself, reached for my keyboard, and banged out my response to Mr. Burnett.

From: barbara@barbaracorcoran.com
Sent: Thursday, December 18, 2008
To: Mark Burnett
Subject: Still Swimming

Mark,

I understand you've asked another girl to dance instead of me. Although I appreciate being reserved as a fallback, I'm much more accustomed to coming in first.

I think you should consider inviting both of us to L.A. for your tryouts. Here are my reasons why:

1. I do my best when my back's against the wall. I love the heat of the competition, as I've learned it brings out my best. I've had all my big successes on the heels of rejection and frankly, it's right up my alley. There was Sister Stella Marie in 5th grade, who said I'd always be stupid because I couldn't read. Then there was the New York old-boy network trying to lock me out of their real estate fortunes, until I became their largest competitor. Then there was the Donald himself, who wrongly swore in court I'd never see a penny of the $4 million commission

he owed me for saving his ass and making the largest land deal in the city's history. And of course there was my ex-partner Ramone Simone, who parted with the words, "You know you'll never succeed without me!" I consider your rejection a lucky charm.

2. If you have both ladies in L.A., you can mix it up a bit and see which personalities make the best combination for your show. I've found in building teams myself that the combination of personalities is always more important than the expertise or strengths of single individuals. You may even drop a man for me because, believe it or not, I'm just as smart and mean as the next guy.

Last, I've known from the get-go the Shark role is a perfect fit for me. Everything I've done so far in the business and TV worlds has made me ready. My style is different than the other Sharks' and your audience would fall in love with me. I've watched thirty-seven dragon episodes so far and know I could rival the best Shark on each show in shrewdness and personality. It seems to me that the same two Sharks steal most of the shows, and I know I'd be one of them.

The reputation you have in your field is equal to the reputation I have in mine, Mark. I know you're the best at what you do and I trust you'll reach the right decision. I've booked my flight for the 6th and hope to be on that plane.

Thanks,

Barbara

I hit the Send button and also had the letter hand-delivered to Mark Burnett in L.A.

When I arrived at the giant Sony Pictures studio lot, I was scared to death. The Hollywood before me looked just like the one I had seen in the movies. There were dozens of gaffers, grips, and technicians running here and there, and it seemed everyone knew exactly what they were doing and where they were going. There were food tables and hot grills serving every kind of food imaginable—all for free—and silver trailers parked everywhere with big gold stars and names on the doors. Someone on the lot was calling my name to start makeup and hair, and when I was done, an assistant came over to escort me to the *Shark Tank* set. When I got there, the male sharks were already seated in their tall leather chairs behind a powerful-looking desk. There was only one chair remaining and I knew it was *hers*.

In one split second, all the heady celebration and confidence I had felt on the plane the night before disappeared. *Poof!* I stood by, waiting for *her* to claim her seat. For a moment I panicked and thought of running away—after all, I knew they really hadn't wanted me there in the first place. Then I realized she wasn't yet there to take the empty chair, so I straightened up, lifted my heavy feet, and stepped onto the set and sat down. Once I was seated, I was never asked to get up and I became the lone female Shark on ABC's new *Shark Tank*.

The men I share the stage with are formidable and all self-made. The handsome one, technology innovator Robert Herjavec, sits to my left. The mean hammerhead shark, financial expert Kevin O'Leary, sits on my immediate right. Next to him is fashion icon Daymond John, who sits next to Kevin Harrington, the infomercial king. Sometimes Kevin Harrington's seat is taken by a visiting Shark. Every Shark there is a millionaire many times over, and it's our cash and the prime-time TV exposure that lure the entrepreneurs into the *Shark Tank*.

In the first ten days of shooting, I heard more than 150 entrepreneurs give their pitches trying to convince us to invest our money in their businesses. All needed our money to make their dream come true. But we don't just give money away; we invest it, and in return we get a chunk of the business. At times, *Shark Tank* is a virtual feeding frenzy as the Sharks compete for a chunk of a fresh idea. But when an entrepreneur presents a bad idea or if he gets greedy, we dismiss it with a curt, "I'm *out!*"

In the first season of *Shark Tank*, I put my hard-earned cash into eight new businesses. Some I landed easily and some I had to snatch out of the jaws of another Shark. I walked into *Shark Tank* having built one hugely successful business, but I expect to leave it having helped build many more.

Here are my tips and tales learned in and out of the *Shark Tank*.

1

Trust Your Gut

When Tiffany Krumins walked onto the *Shark Tank* set, I thought I was looking at a younger me. She had blond hair and bright blue eyes and was holding a small clay elephant in her hands. She had the wide-eyed wonderment and the kind of face that wouldn't see a freight car coming until it had already hit her. From the looks of her, I figured she was a virgin.

Tiffany was a nanny-turned-entrepreneur and I instantly liked how she stepped onto the set, took a deep breath, and turned to look each of us straight in the eye. *This is not a person easily intimidated*, I thought. *This girl is hot stuff!*

Tiffany's new invention was a friendly blue elephant head

with a medicine dropper tucked in its trunk. She pressed its sound button to demonstrate how it worked. The elephant's voice was none other than the sweet voice of the inventor herself. "One, two, *three!*" the elephant cheered. "Open wide. . . . *Good job!*" Tiffany explained that for two years she had been the nanny to a little boy with Down syndrome, and she had designed her elephant to help him more readily take his regular medication. Tiffany held up her blue elephant and promised, "It works every single time. I don't care what your kids hate; they will open up their mouths and smile."

I could see right away by the questions the other Sharks asked that they thought Tiffany was adorable but were *not* taking her or her elephant seriously. They treated her like men do when they're doing a favor for a family friend. But I had a totally different impression of Tiffany and have learned to trust my gut. She sure looked innocent and inexperienced, but I instinctively sensed a backbone made of steel.

I've trusted my gut in every good business decision I've ever made and I decided that choosing my first entrepreneur shouldn't be any different. I moved in for the kill and bought 51 percent of Ava the Elephant, my first *Shark Tank* investment.

None of the other Sharks bid against me, and Kevin O'Leary scoffed at the "outrageous" price of $50,000 for such a "silly business." But the next morning Kevin Harrington's young wife told him, "Men don't have to get up in the middle of the night, trying to get their kids to take their medicine, and you shouldn't have passed on that clever medicine dispenser. Men don't get it, but women will."

Kevin laughed, and I knew for sure my gut had been right.

2

You Can't Fake Passion

I had already committed my cash to seven other businesses in the first ten days of taping and was starting to worry about the potential of losing money. It was the last day of shooting and the worst time for me to hear yet another pitch, so I was quietly repeating to myself over and over, "*Don't* buy any more businesses!"

Pretty Erin Whalen and her muscleman partner, Tim Stansbury, stomped onto the set with a tall stack of bright yellow boxes. Their citrus yellow T-shirts advertised their monkey logo and their product, Grease Monkey Wipes. They began their pitch: "Grease Monkey Wipes are individually wrapped, all-natural citrus degreasing wipes that can degrease an entire bicycle, the chain, and your hands with just *one* wipe!"

I liked them both immediately and also the great packaging of their product. But with only two more pitches to go, I was determined to keep my money in my pocket. "Don't buy; don't buy," I kept repeating to myself. But when pretty-boy Shark Robert Herjavec circled in to take a chomp out of their business, I got jealous and just had to take a juicy bite, too. I liked Erin's enthusiasm and thought Grease Monkey Wipes a clear winner.

As Robert went to close his deal, I interrupted. "Just a minute. I might jump in there for a piece, too." *What the heck*, I thought, *spending another $20,000 won't put me in the poorhouse.* I couldn't stand missing a good opportunity. "Tell me something, Erin and Tim. I'm sitting here having a hard time parting with my money because I don't want to lose it. Tell me *why* I should risk losing it by investing in your monkey business."

Erin immediately stepped in close to the *Shark Tank* desk, with a smile that even the devil would trust, and spoke with conviction. "We are very, very passionate about this," she said, "and want to create a global-wide empire. I promise if you partner with us, we will *not* let you down. I promise you, Barbara, we will make this work. *I promise.*"

Erin had enough passion in her plea to send legions of soldiers right off a cliff. She reminded me a lot of Emily O'Sullivan, my Chanel-clad powerhouse salesperson at The Corcoran Group. I ended my first interview with Emily so many years ago with my signature "I don't think you're aggressive" challenge, my surefire system to pick out a winner. When Emily vehemently reacted to my challenge by practically leaping across the desk to strangle me, I knew I had a winner. I figured Erin was cut out of the same cloth.

"I'm *in*!" I said, reaching across the desk to shake my new partner's hand.

Back in my New York office, before signing the deal, I met with Erin and Tim. Tim relayed to me that it was *he* who was the lead partner of Grease Monkey Wipes, as he single-handedly managed the Web site, was the company's blogger, made the sales calls to the bike shops, and personally handled all the shipping. I listened carefully and knew the moment had come to try my old insult trick. I decided to start with Tim.

"I've listened hard today, Tim," I said, "and I've concluded that your business is really just a nice hobby. I'm sure you'll have a lot of fun doing it and make new friends and a few bucks along the way, but Grease Monkey Wipes is just not the kind of product that could ever become a *real* business, wouldn't you agree?" Tim was in total agreement and went on to tell me about how much fun he and Erin were already having promoting their wipes on the weekend biking circuit.

I glanced over at Erin and, although they weren't married, Erin looked like a woman who would be serving Tim with divorce papers that afternoon. "With all due respect, Barbara," she said, "you're absolutely *wrong*! Grease Monkey Wipes is *definitely* a business, and I will *not* be happy until I make Grease

Monkey Wipes a nationally successful brand and company sold in every store in America."

And that was exactly the passion I wanted to hear. I knew Erin would prove a phenomenal partner, and along with Tim's acumen for detail, together we would be able to build a big business. I quickly signed the deal and made a mental note to work on what would be our first business challenge—how best to move Erin from second to lead dog.

3

Dress the Part

Gayla Bentley and her entourage of women stormed the *Shark Tank* set, dressed to kill. They were all decked out in original Gayla Bentley designs, a perfect walking billboard for plus-size women. She was a powerhouse to be reckoned with; I knew she would leave the tank with either a pound of flesh or a pile of cash, and I was hoping it wasn't going to be mine.

Gayla was no newcomer to the fashion world, having built a successful boutique in Dallas selling her chubby couture. She planted her hands squarely on her hips and in a booming voice better suited for the army cut right to the chase: "My name is Gayla Bentley and I am the designer and founder of the Gayla Bentley Fashion Design Group and I am here tonight to ask you for your wisdom and your experience . . . and $250,000 for a 20 percent equity stake in my company. I represent 60 percent of the American women, who wear a size 12 or larger. You know us; we're your neighbor, your sister, your friend. And we are *tired* of being discriminated against—being forced to shop in the far corners of the department stores only to find clothes that don't fit and that we don't like!"

Gayla had great charisma and I knew her personality would hit a chord with every plus-size woman in America. She also dressed the part, which is essential for succeeding in business. I never regretted blowing my first commission check on my fancy Bergdorf coat, and wore it up and down the streets of Manhattan feeling like the million bucks I didn't yet have. It forced me to measure up to a whole new image, and whether or not my customers liked my coat, I at least looked successful enough to buy it. Wearing it, I felt ready to take on the world, and that's exactly what I did.

All the best money I spent in business was on the things that helped create an image of success. I copied the typeface of the famous Tiffany store for my first business card and used gray ink, at no extra charge, instead of the usual black. I rented my pink Princess phone, one dollar extra per month, because I felt just like a fancy business lady every time I answered the phone.

When it comes to building a successful business, I've

learned to fake it till you make it—you've got to dress the part.

When I committed my money to Gayla and her team, she turned to her plus-size beauties, raised both arms in celebration, and declared, "Okay, girls, let's *eat!*"

4

Do Your Homework

Brett Thompson and Heath Hall were working on the floor of the U.S. Senate debating pork barrel spending when they decided to launch their barbecue sauce business on weekends. "We've decided to take useless pork barrel spending," Heath told us, "and put our money to good use and create our new company, Pork Barrel BBQ."

Their *Shark Tank* appearance on national prime-time TV got them the money they needed and enough overnight notoriety to land a big distributor and a Pork Barrel restaurant chain in Washington, D.C.

The two good ol' boys came onto the set and hit the floor running. Their years as attorneys pitching pork barrel spending to old, jaded senators had well prepared them for meeting the

Sharks. They gave us their pitch in easy-to-follow logic with every detail in place, and when we bombarded them with our questions, it was obvious they had taken the time to think through every possible answer. Brett and Heath were clearly over-prepared, and even though I don't like barbecue sauce, I couldn't wait to hand the boys my cash.

I have never met a really smart person who didn't over-prepare, and after flunking my audition for the high school cheerleading squad because I hadn't bothered to learn the cheers, I swore to myself that I would never be caught unprepared again. I find that my over-preparation and the insecurity that drives it have always guaranteed my success.

Sometimes very successful people appear to be winging it, because they look so comfortable on their feet. But don't be fooled; there ain't no such thing. They just come across that way because they practiced so many times. Doing your homework well takes time—time less successful people aren't willing to give. Putting the extra effort into preparation results in extra rewards in the execution.

5

Fancy Talk Don't Work

Nothing about Dan Mackey was fancy. He stood there ready to pitch with thumbs hooked in his jeans pockets. There was a stack of soda cans lined up on a table behind him. Dan had to be the most unassuming entrepreneur we had heard yet, and he handed out sample flavors of his soda in small paper cups while delivering his all-natural Chill Soda pitch. He was a low-key Californian and seemed confident he had a sure winner on his hands if only he could get the needed money for his first soda run.

Dan's pitch was straightforward and he delivered it in five minutes flat: "I made a soda that not only tastes great, it's also 100 percent natural! All organic, low glycemic." Dan said he didn't think his nephew should be drinking the sugared sodas available in school vending machines and that he had worked long and hard in making his all-natural soda a reality. He had set his sights on selling it to the California school system and had already landed a big distributor to help sell it.

Dan's single best trait was his total lack of pretension. He kept his pitch plain and simple, like his soda. No other Sharks were interested in putting their cash into a soda business; they said the odds of winning were one in a thousand. Kevin O'Leary was dismissive, riddling Dan with questions, but Dan remained unflustered and easily stood his ground. All Dan's answers were short, and I trusted him because he was such a clean communicator. I put my $50,000 on the table.

The next month Dan arrived in my New York office to sign the contract with his fancy new partner-CEO in tow. With one quick look at the CEO's power suit, I figured it had set him back about a thousand bucks. Dan's new guy spent two hours telling me what Dan had been able to say on *Shark Tank* in five minutes. His words were sophisticated and my phony-baloney barometer was beeping in overdrive. I kept thinking about my $50,000 and how quickly this new CEO would spend it.

I don't have a business degree—I'm lucky I got out of college—but I've always had enough common sense not to fall for big words and puffery. Dan's CEO reminded me a lot of the powerful Mr. Milstein and his highfalutin pitch years earlier to buy my company. Mr. Milstein had talked on and on of synergies, market share, diminishing returns, and a lot of other things

I wasn't educated enough to know about or care about, but I was smart enough to say no to his offer.

You can bet the more fancy somebody talks, the less capable he is. It's easy to recognize when someone's being genuine, but fancy talk can be a smokescreen and a distraction from the stuff that really matters. I've often put my money on the D student over the guy with the MBA, because the D student isn't smart enough to hide things in fancy words and usually has more common sense.

When Dan's CEO finished his swanky presentation with the usual braggadocio about having all the right connections in all the right places, I decoded the true meaning of all the fancy words, and it was this: "You gave us $50,000 already, but what we *really* need is a few million dollars, and we'd like to take it with us today."

I already knew my answer, plain and simple: "No." I wouldn't give another penny until the CEO could show me real results. I had learned long ago that overstaters *always* underperform.

6

Pushy People Deliver

When Cactus Jack stood on the set, he was a shimmering white sight to behold! The six-foot, 273-pound Iowa cowboy wore a ten-gallon hat, white leather pants, a satin shirt with fringed sleeves, and rhinestone-studded boots. Cactus told us right out that he was an inventor with as many flops as successes to his credit, and he bragged about his 1-Shot All Purpose Cleaner, the invention that had made him *rich*.

Cactus was fresh out of cash and needed $180,000 to make an infomercial to launch his new exercise machine, the Body Jac. It weighed less than fifteen pounds and was designed to help guys with fat guts do push-ups. With his own huge belly bulging over his rhinestone belt, Cactus looked nothing like a guy who should be selling exercise equipment.

Cactus Jack seemed to consider himself at least equal to the Sharks he was pitching for money. We weren't biting, and worse, Kevin O'Leary was treating him like an old person whose glory days were long gone. He cut the cowboy down to size by saying, "Your Body Jac will *never* succeed and you know it, Jack!" But Cactus was a natural-born salesman and simply didn't listen. He kept talking and reminded me a lot of the pushiest salesperson I had ever worked with: Carrie Chiang. Carrie didn't listen and was impatient and unbelievably annoying. But as result she was a superstar dealmaker and had made me many millions of dollars over the years at The Corcoran Group, including closing the largest land sale in New York City's history: fourteen city blocks owned by an even more annoying character, Donald Trump. I regularly tortured Carrie by telling her that someone else at the office was making more money than she, and time and again she took the bait and sold another five million dollars' worth of property to prove me wrong.

I liked Cactus Jack for his persistence and pushiness, and I also liked his Body Jac. I decided I'd jump in only if I could get Shark Kevin Harrington to jump in with me. Kevin was the infomercial king and the person I'd most need to get an infomercial on the air. Without Kevin in the mix, I figured I'd have to deal with Cactus myself, which I already knew I didn't want to do; I made a mental note to make that Kevin's job later.

I presented Jack with a challenge: "Listen here, Cactus Jack. I'll give you *half* of the $180,000 investment, if you can wrestle the other half from Kevin Harrington. But even if you do, you're a sorry state of a salesman, trying to pass yourself off as a health guru. You're *fat*, Jack, and can't even see your cowboy boots past your own belly! So my cash offer is also contingent on you losing thirty pounds in thirty days."

Cynical Kevin O'Leary weighed in with, "I've got news for you, guy. There's no chance in hell you're losing thirty pounds. This deal is never going to happen. The thirty pounds is going to keep it off the table—*forever*."

One month later, Cactus had lost his thirty pounds, and by year's end, he had succeeded in annoying enough people to get his infomercial produced and on air in record time. Kevin, Cactus, and I have been selling Body Jacs on TV ever since.

None of my *Shark Tank* partners has proved as pushy or as lovable as my cowboy from Iowa. Cactus is definitely a royal pain in the ass, but he's also the kind of partner I never check up on or worry about, because I know he's raising holy hell on my behalf should anything in our business fall off track. I fully expect Cactus to make more money for me than Carrie Chiang ever did.

7

You Gotta Have a Gimmick

Excuse me, Heath," I said to the president of Pork Barrel BBQ sauce. He was standing center stage under the bright lights and *Shark Tank* cameras. "Has anyone ever told you that you bear a remarkable resemblance to an adorable pig?" I was thinking he resembled the pink pig face in the center of his Pork Barrel BBQ sauce logo. "I have to say I can't look at you without picturing you in a pig costume as your company's mascot. You're a very handsome man and I'm not saying you *look* like a pig; I'm saying you'd look adorable as a real live pig!"

Heath shifted uncomfortably, obviously embarrassed. "I guess I'll take that as a compliment," he rang back.

Kevin O'Leary, always the meanest Shark on set, surprised me by raising his hands in protest. "Barbara," he said, "are you actually telling this man that he *looks like a pig*?!" But I was just stating the obvious and didn't see the coincidence as a negative at all, but as a *huge* marketing advantage! I was thinking about Frank Perdue and his famous Perdue chickens and how lucky he was to have been born looking like a chicken. And he had built the biggest chicken business in America. I figured there must be a thousand or so barbecue brands out there, but not one could make claim to an owner who looked like a pig. Heath stiffened again as dozens of cameramen and lighting guys watched to see what might happen next.

"I'll tell you what, Heath," I pushed on. "If you'd be willing to wear a pig suit when promoting and selling your barbecue sauce, I'd like to be your partner. We could have a home run hit with the potential to out-market every other barbecue sauce out there." Heath's partner, Brett, looked excited and got it right away, nodding in agreement. Easy for him, I thought, considering *he* wasn't the one who was going to have to dress like a pig. We all waited for Heath's answer, and I hoped he was taking my offer seriously.

"So, Heath," I said. "What do you say? I'll give you $50,000 for 50 percent of your business, with the contingency that you dress as a pig."

Heath paused, picturing his future life. "Why, ma'am," he finally said with easy, down-home charm, "I believe we have ourselves a deal!" I believed we'd make ourselves a fortune.

After the *Shark Tank* episode aired, everyone responded to

Heath's natural-born gimmick. That weekend Brett and Heath drove a thirty-foot silver trailer called Pork Barrel One to New York City and served two fifteen-pound briskets, four huge pork butts, twenty chicken quarters, and eight slabs of ribs to *Fox & Friends* fans for three hours with millions of viewers watching on TV. Over the next twelve months, Pork Barrel BBQ sauce would be carried in one thousand stores nationwide.

I first learned the power of a good gimmick when competing with Gloria and her attention-grabbing breasts at the Fort Lee Diner. The red ribbons I tied to my pigtails worked like a dream and my tips almost doubled. After that, I used lots of gimmicks to build my brand, the first being my "1 BEDROOM PLUS DEN" advertisement that made my one-bedroom apartment outshine all the other ho-hum one-bedrooms out there. It was a gimmick that gave my little business a fast start, and I knew the Pork Barrel BBQ brand would get the same fast start by using Heath Hall as their gimmick.

Good salesmanship is never anything more than playing up the positives and minimizing the negatives, and if you can find a unique gimmick, it will give you a huge leg up over your competitors.

8

Everybody Wants What Everybody Wants

Miracles happen when an entrepreneur is featured on *Shark Tank*. Often overnight they are wooed by stores wanting to buy their product, besieged by eager consumers asking where they can buy it and investors who suddenly want in—typically the same ones who had no interest the week before.

One thing I've learned in building my own business is that everybody wants what everybody wants—and nobody wants what nobody wants. My One Day, One Price sale of eighty-eight unwanted apartments is a perfect example. The week before the sale, those eighty-eight apartments were considered the dregs of the market, having gone unsold for more than three years. But once I had set a deadline and created a sense of urgency by pricing them all alike, I created a buying frenzy overnight, selling all the units in one day and putting a happy million dollars in my pocket, saving my company from bankruptcy. When the last apartment sold, there were another fifty buyers waiting in line, making the guy who got the runt of the litter feel lucky.

When customers are told they *can't* have something, you can bet they'll always want it more. But tell the same customers you have plenty to go around, and they go home to think about it. I wouldn't invest in nearly as many businesses on *Shark Tank* as I do if not for the four other greedy Sharks sitting around me. If an entrepreneur gets one Shark interested, other Sharks almost always want to feed, too. And fans at home love the competition. Many tell me their greatest thrill is watching me beat out another Shark for a deal—the more blood in the water, the better.

Prime-time TV exposure is the magic dust that makes everyone interested. After Erin and Tim, of Grease Monkey Wipes, appeared on *Shark Tank*, their orders and Web visits increased by more than 8,000 percent. The morning following their appearance they were the number one search on Google and remained one of the top three searches for the next two days. When I challenged Cactus Jack to lose thirty pounds, Nutrisystem called asking him to be their new poster child for weight loss. They were willing to promote his Body Jac in their ads. Gayla Bentley had been knocking on doors for twenty years, but when she showcased her fashions on *Shark Tank*, the Stage stores became the first national retailer to carry her line. When

Tiffany Krumins showcased her little elephant, CVS, the giant pharmaceutical chain, ordered fifteen thousand.

Everybody wants what everybody wants. And if there is no demand for your product, you've got to find a way to create the illusion that there is.

9

Step Apart from the Crowd

Heath Hall and Brett Thompson, of Pork Barrel BBQ, are two of the best promoters I've ever met. They have an uncanny ability to get themselves noticed and make themselves heard. After appearing on *Shark Tank*, Heath and Brett had a 5,000 percent increase in Web traffic to porkbarrelbbq.com. Yes, 5,000 percent! They quickly parlayed their newfound notoriety into many other TV appearances resulting in tons of press coverage. Needless to say, their sales have gone through the roof.

By growing up in a family with ten kids, I learned how to grab attention in a crowded market. Our house gave me the training I needed to later compete for the limelight in a crowded city of eight million people. Getting publicity for your company is nothing more than finding a way to step out and grab some attention.

Contrary to common belief, the most effective way to build a brand is not by spending millions in advertising, but by finding a clever way to keep your name in the press. After the Catholic miracle of my *Corcoran Report* appearing on the front page of the *New York Times* with me quoted as the expert, I realized that providing a statistical report to the press was the slam dunk of all good publicity. I continued to churn out reports for the next thirty years.

Information that might seem mundane to you because you work with it day in and day out can become the basis of a good story. The figures you know well aren't boring to an outsider who knows little about your business. If you're smart enough to package your own industry facts and figures into a simple statistical report, you're bound to make news, as reporters base many of their stories on statistics.

I was happy I named *The Corcoran Report* after myself. I was self-conscious initially, since I was a nobody in my industry and knew my name didn't add any credibility. I was even afraid it would work against my report, but I was wrong. By putting my name on it, I became the expert and built my name brand.

My first *Corcoran Report* was one page long and simply provided prices for apartment sales by neighborhood. Heath and Brett now publish the *Pork Barrel Report* and keep it simple, too. This one-page list of the top five most wasteful projects passed by Congress, such as the "$16 million on canned pork for $1.99 a pound that usually sells for $1" and "$6.4 billion awarded to congressional districts that don't even exist," is sure to get their brand publicity.

When I published my first report, it was based only on the eleven sales I had made. My salespeople were against it and rightfully argued that my eleven sales was not a large enough basis to arrive at an average sale price for *all* of New York City. They warned that our company would totally lose credibility, but what they didn't realize was that we had no credibility. The way I saw it, we had nothing to lose and nowhere to go but up. I learned to ignore well-meaning naysayers, even though they're often the people who care about you the most. *The Corcoran Report*, published too early with insufficient information, made my company stand out and get noticed. It's never too early to publish a report.

I made sure I got our report out every six months without fail. Most of my competitors soon copied it with one of their own, but they were never consistent in getting it out. The reporters quickly learned to rely on me for industry information because my data was always ready.

Through good times and bad, I was the expert in my industry who was always quoted. I was trusted by the newspapers because I always told it like it was. Every time the stock market fell in New York City, Manhattan apartment prices fell with it. And as my competitors ran for cover, not wanting to report bad news, I took the bad news to the media as quickly as I could. When I reported that the market was turning around for the better, they covered that story, too, because they believed me.

When my husband, Bill Higgins, wants to reach me, he says he's calling from the *New York Times* and knows I'll immediately pick up the phone. I've learned that the first person the reporter reaches on a story he's writing inevitably gets the quote. If you're the second person reached, you'll be stuck confirming your competitor's quote.

People who get quoted know how to talk short. Although I feel more intelligent espousing to a reporter with a lengthy answer to a question, I've learned lengthy answers never get quoted. You're much better off if you learn how to talk like the average Joe. "Yep, the market sucks!" is sure to get quoted.

If an entrepreneur builds his business thinking the best way to get noticed is by spending money on advertising, he's overlooking the most powerful tool in brand building: the power of the press. Publicity is the easiest and cheapest way to have your business step apart from the crowd.

10

Expand Before You're Ready

I expanded my company much like my parents grew their family. Mom would announce, "Eddie, I'm pregnant," and Dad would run out to get another bed. I grew The Corcoran Group from six to sixty salespeople in its first five years because I learned that the secret to growing your business fast is not waiting until you're ready.

With each business I've bought into on *Shark Tank*, the most successful ones expand before they're ready. When Erin and Tim, of Grease Monkey Wipes, won their $40,000 investment from Shark Robert Herjavec and me, they were peddling individually wrapped wipes to bike stores in their local area. But before the cash even hit their hands, they went out to design a new sixty-wipe canister version of their original product, enabling them to go after the larger and more lucrative automotive market. Less successful entrepreneurs wait and enjoy what comes easily, but not Erin and Tim. They were smart enough to see our cash infusion for what it was—opportunity knocking—and they quickly used it to bang down some new doors.

Heath and Brett, my BBQ boys, also quickly built their brand, creating two new products in their first year of business: a sweeter version of their BBQ sauce and an all-natural, non-GMO BBQ sauce. Just like other entrepreneurs who dream of putting their product in every store in America, they knew they needed more products, or "SKUs," to attract a large distributor. So instead of just selling more of their same sauce, they used my money to go whole hog and create the new products, giving them access to the lucrative Whole Foods and Costco stores.

Don't believe the children's tale about the hare and the tortoise. I've found the businesses that always win the race are the ones that jump fast and run for the finish line. I created a couple of good habits to grow my business. First, even though I never had enough room for every person I wanted to hire, when a good person walked through the door, I always found a spot to put her. I divided my conference room four times at The Corcoran Group to squeeze more people in and chopped my own office in half twice. And second, I opened every new office two years too soon, while my competitors sat back waiting for the perfect time. Sure, it's easier to follow the pack, but all the best turf is already claimed by the time you get there. Taking more space than you actually need is the business equivalent of putting a gun to your own head. It always forced me to move faster, think quicker, and find a way to pay the rent.

Good entrepreneurship is all about staying on the move. Every successful entrepreneur I work with expands before he's ready. It's the best formula I know for aggressive growth and the best way to become the market leader.

11

Be Willing to Flop

If you want to see a picture of failure, take a look at Cactus Jack. If you want to see a picture of success, take an even closer look. Cactus Jack has invented more than fifty products over his sixty-seven years on this good earth. His most successful creation is the 1-Shot All Purpose Cleaner, which has grossed more than $10 million in sales and put $3 million in his pocket. His list of less successful inventions is long—the Stain King, the World Class Arm Wrestling Machine, and Uncle Tug, his newfangled electronic tug-of-war machine—but they were all dead on arrival. Cactus Jack simply wasn't afraid to fail.

The Corcoran Group became the innovator in my industry because I was always willing to fail. Most of my innovations were built on a leap and a prayer, using money I should never have spent in the first place. I think of a new idea as a small white bird flying by, and if I don't grab it right then, it's gone a moment later. I learned there is no better time to bring the idea to life than at the very moment of its inception. I also learned that the surefire way to kill an idea is to send it to a committee or an attorney for review.

All my best ideas came from talking to the little guy. It was our receptionist who thought of our successful Powerbroker advertising campaign. I copied my One Day, One Price sale from the farmer's puppy sale. I was able to sell an unsalable building because a mailroom clerk was smart enough to suggest that I paint the building pink and label it the "pink elephant."

Being afraid to fail stops you from trying things in the first place. I learned after many failures that nobody's watching and nobody gives a damn. If you want to build a successful business, you don't have to get it right; you just have to get it going.

12

Shoot the Dogs Early

We had the happiest and most productive real estate firm in town because we hired the best people, compensated them well, and went out of our way to show appreciation. That was the fun part. But I also learned that to keep my company healthy and happy, I had to shoot the dogs early!

Firing people is the worst part of running any business, but I got good at it. When I spot a chronic complainer, I can't wait to fire him, as one complainer quickly recruits another to join his pity party, and that will rot a business faster than anything else. People who are usually good at hiring are terrible at firing and procrastinate for far too long, because firing someone is also an admission that you hired the wrong person in the first place. And people don't readily admit to being wrong.

Every business sells a product or service, so they are reliant on its sales force. If you keep a desk filled with the wrong person, you can easily deceive yourself into thinking the desk is productive simply because someone is sitting there.

I made it a standing policy at The Corcoran Group to clean out the bottom 25 percent of my sales force every year. My pink bunny shoes were just a gimmick to encourage my managers to get the job done. I knew if the bottom quarter of my sales force was not earning their keep, I had far less money to support the amazing people on top making all the money. As the company leader, I saw it as part of my job to eliminate the deadwood and get people on their way to a career that suited them better.

If you have to let someone go, I've developed some ways to make that process a bit friendlier. When I sit down to break the bad news, I make it a point to have someone else with me for moral support. I always had Esther at my side at The Corcoran Group because I was afraid of chickening out, but with Esther there, I was accountable for getting the job done.

I like to open the good-bye meeting with the same question: "Do you mind if I'm honest with you?" I want the person's permission to tell him right away that the job is not working out. As I've been fired from a lot of jobs myself, I can tell you it's bad enough being fired, but it's even more painful sitting there wondering why you're there in the first place. The person being fired never wants to spend a lot of time discussing it, so I tell him what I need to say and keep the good-bye short.

I always tell the truth, because everyone deserves to know what they've done wrong. It's simply not fair to leave people wondering. I also make a point of telling people exactly what they've done well in their jobs. It allows them to leave with their self-esteem intact, and if you take the time to commend them for what they do well, it's easier for them to accept your criticism. Most important, it helps them find a new job that better suits their talents.

On *Shark Tank* I don't have a lot of time to size people up. I'm forced to make a quick judgment about each entrepreneur I meet on set, and I've made some mistakes. I commit to every business I want in good faith, hoping and praying the entrepreneur will show good faith in return. I've often found entrepreneurs overstate, misrepresent, or flat-out lie about important details. Some don't have the patent they claimed to have or the sales orders they bragged about, or their "excellent credit" reads more like a bankruptcy. One young woman even forgot to mention the ex-husband who actually owned her business! I'm often amazed.

Once I leave the *Shark Tank* set, I head back to New York on a heated mission to ferret out the truths and non-truths of what's been represented to me on camera. In short, I'm out to shoot the dogs early. I've developed my own due diligence process, disguised as a friendly "welcome package." It has twenty simple questions bound to get to the root of any problem. My questions uncover hidden partners, bad debt, and sometimes even time spent in prison. If you're planning to come into the *Shark Tank* or go into a successful business venture with anyone, you'd better be prepared to hang your underwear out on the line.

13

Fun Is Good Business

Not everyone has a place dedicated solely to fun, but Cactus Jack has a cabin on the Iowa-Missouri border and he calls it his "little Disneyland." His cabin is decorated all year long in Christmas lights because he says it gives him bright ideas. Stuffed elk, deer, and bear heads hang on the wall, along with the largest Pez collection in the world. He rides around on an old tractor that has a set of water buffalo horns strapped on the front.

Cactus likes to brag about never having had a job in his life. He also doesn't have an office, yet he's the inventor of more than fifty products and has twelve patents to his name. Jack thought of every invention while playing outside or just messing around. One of his biggest moneymakers—his 1-Shot Catch Alot Fishing System—was invented on a fishing trip right after he saw the movie *Jaws*. The system has a lure with a secret compartment that releases chum to attract fish, just like he saw in the movie. I'm Jack's partner on his fifty-first product, the Body Jac, and I'm sure it won't be his last.

I built my company on pure fun, and believe that fun is the most underutilized motivational tool in business today. All of my best ideas came when I was playing outside the office with the people I worked with. We thought of everything from our best advertising and publicity ideas to whole new ways of doing business while we were outside. Many of the fun things we did away from the office we brought back with us, like our in-office massages, manicures, yoga classes, and Ping-Pong tables.

I always worked hard to make our fun times really special and thought of it as spoiling my children. I bused six hundred people to the country for midweek picnics and made sure each of the picnics had a great gimmick. One had a sixty-foot hot-air balloon waiting in the backyard to take people for a ride, another had a five-thousand-pound elephant and a spitting camel waiting on the front lawn to offer safari rides, and for yet another I leased ten Thoroughbreds in full regalia, which we all raced up and down the back fields.

People most resistant to fun need it the most, and I've found that all they need is a little encouragement. Our most proper Park Avenue ladies were the first to hike up their skirts and hop on the back of the Harley-Davidsons when a gang of tattooed guys roared up onto the lawn at one infamous picnic.

I had our Sweetheart Party near Valentine's Day each year because February was the coldest and most depressing month. And since companies don't plan parties in February, I got all the best venues in town at half price. I changed the theme every year to keep the party fresh, and no one got in without a costume.

I opened our Stars on Broadway party in a 42nd Street theater dressed as Carol Channing lip-synching "Hello, Dolly!" and the party was an immediate success. At our Dress in Drag party, every one of our eight hundred men and women cross-dressed, and we laughed about it for years to come. For the Glamorous '40s party, high atop Rockefeller Plaza, I wore nothing more than a girdle, a pink vintage bra, and seamed stockings, with an ice pack pinned to my head. I stuffed my 46DD bra with two softballs and got more kisses and gropes from my staff than I had gotten in the previous ten years of my marriage. Good themes make parties more fun—the more ridiculous, the more fun everyone has. And please, please don't have a company Christmas party with everyone in business attire. Believe me, nobody will have fun.

Conducting business as usual always results in usual business, but if a company plans good times together, it can result in extraordinary business! What I got in return for the enormous effort I put into planning fun for my company was not only extreme loyalty, but the most profitable real estate company per person in the United States.

14

Pick Good People

I look for the same three traits in every entrepreneur I choose to do business with: good character, lots of enthusiasm, and a genuine sense of thankfulness. On *Shark Tank*, I'll often bet on the right person in the wrong business because I know she'll find a way to reinvent the business and make it a success. Picking the right person is the crucial foundation of every deal I do.

My first chance to size someone up is the moment she walks onto the *Shark Tank* set. Before that, I've never met the entrepreneur. I don't have any information about the business or the product.

When the entrepreneur arrives at the studio, she is instructed to walk through the Shark tunnel to her mark center stage. She's been told to stand there and not to speak until one of the Sharks speak to her. But what she doesn't know is that the Sharks have been told not to say a word to her for a full five minutes. So we all sit there staring down from our big raised desk, watching the behind-the-scenes trick planned to put pressure on the unsuspecting entrepreneur.

The entrepreneur is baffled as to why no one is talking to her, often shaking at the knees and sweating her stage makeup off, as a half dozen giant cameras circle around her. The close-up camera comes within ten inches of everyone's face to capture every twitch of the eye. What the show gets out of these five grueling minutes is real human drama and great television. What I get is my first impression of someone's character, a chance to size up how well she handles real pressure. Is she comfortable? Is she looking me in the eye? Would I leave my kid with her for five years and come back to find my kid okay? What I'm looking for is a good person who will make a good partner.

As Cactus Jack stood in front of the Sharks for his five-minute silent treatment, it was *Jack* who was intimidating! With his big squared shoulders and oversize cowboy hat, he looked like a gunslinger getting ready to take his ten paces, aim, and fire. He leveled his gaze on each Shark with a confidence we could all plainly see. From the way he was dressed, Jack was clearly a character, but he also looked to me like a man of *good* character, and I trusted him before he even started his pitch. Once Cactus Jack became my business partner, his stand-up way of doing business proved my instincts right. I learned to respect his word, as when we first shook hands on the deal and he shouted, "Cactus Jack, he's your man! If *he* can't do it, *nobody* can!"

When Gayla Bentley stormed the set, her engine was already in full throttle. Her energy was off the charts, and I could feel it eight feet away. Although she stood on her mark as instructed, she smiled and flirted with each of us, using only her eyes. Once Gayla began her sales pitch, it was obvious she could sell anything. When Kevin O'Leary hammered her with his usual aggressive questions, she easily stood her ground, looking tougher than Kevin ever could. She was pure energy from the moment she arrived until she left the stage, and after she exited, she left a puff of happiness behind her. Watching Gayla's energized performance, I knew she had the needed oomph to build a very successful business.

Every good partner I've had is genuinely thankful. Once I gave Tiffany Krumins the money she needed to make her elephant mold, get her patent, and manufacture her product, she expressed her appreciation in every conversation we had. Then fate put her character to the test. A few weeks after her *Shark Tank* appearance, Tiffany was diagnosed with a deadly cancer, but managed to build her business from her hospital bed. Through a torturous year of surgery and chemotherapy, she got her patent and mold finished, designed her packaging, and located the best manufacturer in China to produce her elephant. She stayed focused and remained thankful. People who come through in the end always have rock-solid character.

Young Tiffany miraculously followed through with her first order, fifteen-thousand-pieces for CVS, one year after she began her fight with cancer.

If you're going to build a big business, sooner or later you have to hire the right people to help you run it, and when you do, you'd better pick them carefully. I've hired many people since I chose my first good partner, Esther Kaplan. Since then, I've learned a few things about how to pick good ones.

The best people have the essential qualities of character, energy, and thankfulness. If someone lacks integrity, you'll find he won't be there for you when the going gets tough. If someone is apathetic, he won't make it to the finish line. And if someone is not appreciative at the onset, you can count on the fact that he'll stab you in the back later when there's real money on the table.

I'm sitting on the *Shark Tank* set always looking for a good business to invest in, but I'm really looking for something far more important. I'm looking for a person I can trust with my money, my reputation, and my time.

This Tale's End

I'm on a plane to Los Angeles and once again can barely sit still in my seat. I'm off to tape the next season of *Shark Tank*, and by this time tomorrow, I'll be back in my big leather chair. I close my eyes for a minute and think about my life-long adventure and how I made it here.

I smile remembering it was Nana Henwood who actually predicted my destiny so long ago. Besides being almost a midget, my nana also had the honor of being our personal bedtime masseuse, spending a few minutes every night with each of her ten grandchildren. I vividly recall the night Nana found me crying. I was hiding my arms beneath my covers.

"Let me see your arms," she coaxed.

"No!" I said. "They look just like Dad's."

Nana gently pulled my arms out from the covers and proudly announced, "*Hairy arms*! That means you're going to be *rich*!"

A few years later, hoping to fulfill my nana's prophecy, I got my first job as a summer playground supervisor. By the time I turned twenty-four, I had tried twenty-two others. Finally, my twenty-fourth job actually made me rich.

How did I get here? First, I believed my nana's words. More important, I used what I learned from my mother.

I was once young, broke, and ambitious, too, and I see a piece of myself in every entrepreneur I meet. I don't really think of myself as a "shark." It's a label I would have never given myself. I like to think I built my success on hard work, common sense, and playing nice.

So far, I've had an *amazing* ride and figure I have about fifteen good years left. I plan to use those years helping as many people hit the jackpot as I can. I can't wait to see what's next.

Best of luck

Barbara

Whatever Happened To . . .

★ **. . . Mom and Dad?**

Florence and Ed retired to Florida. Dad relaxes in his La-Z-Boy watching his big-screen TV, and Mom washes beach towels for her visiting twenty-six grandchildren.

★ **. . . Ramòne Simòne?**

Ray and Tina remain happily married, have three children, and live in suburban New York. The Pogue-Simone Company closed in the early 1980s.

★ **. . . Gloria and the Fort Lee Diner?**

Gloria bought herself a pink Cadillac Eldorado and retired with her two well-rounded friends to Virginia. The Fort Lee Diner on Main Street is now the New Magic Wok Chinese Restaurant.

☆ . . . *Palisades Amusement Park?*

Irvin Rosenthal sold his amusement park and his stretch limo in the 1960s. The Caterpillar, the Giant Cyclone, and the world's largest saltwater pool were replaced with twelve hundred condominium apartments.

☆ . . . *Maggie O'Shay?*

Until her death in 1992, Mrs. O'Shay continued to pace up and down Undercliff Avenue minding everyone else's business. People regularly report sightings of her still inspecting Edgewater's lovely front yards.

☆ . . . *John Campagna?*

My first landlord sold his apartment building and moved to Arizona. He e-mailed me after my first book was published to say, "It wasn't my idea to evict you; it was the super's, Charlie O'Rourke!"

☆ . . . *Sister Stella Marie?*

She terrorized the Holy Rosary School until 1962, when she left Edgewater. She died in 1994 and is buried at Holy Cross Cemetery in North Arlington, New Jersey. May she rest in peace.

☆ . . . *Esther Kaplan?*

Esther retired as the president of The Corcoran Group in

2001. She is wealthy and lives in New York City near her children and grandchildren. She teaches adults how to read in her spare time and still carries the most organized purse in town.

✲ *. . . Bill Higgins?*

After years of counseling, Bill and I are still happily married. Bill dabbled in teaching math and science in a Bronx elementary school and is now coaching our son and daughter in after-school sports, causing his knees to be replaced.

✲ *. . . Dad's Blue Beauty?*

Denise learned how to drive in Dad's prized Chevy station wagon, slamming the back end into the window of the Hackensack Bridal Shop and forcing Dad to buy fourteen bridal gowns. Next, Eddie learned to drive in the dented station wagon, demolishing the front end by driving it through the plate glass window of Hiram's Roadstand, a hot dog joint in Fort Lee.

✲ *. . . Ron Rossi?*

Ron skated his way to great sales success and landed The Corcoran Group's first million-dollar listing in 1980. He was the first person we lost to the AIDS epidemic and his style and fun-loving spirit are still missed.

★   *. . . Charlie's boat?*

Charlie, the old Swede, took down the old shed in 1961, towed his sailboat to the Edgewater Marina, and sailed away.

★   *. . . the Donald?*

After his failed bid for President of the United States, the Donald and his puffed blond helmet have moved on to a new career in television and movies.

★   *. . . Carrie Chiang?*

Selling more than $100 million in real estate every year, Carrie holds her title as New York City's top condominium broker. She still calls me Baa-bwa.

★   *. . . Chicky Dayock?*

The elegant Mrs. Dayock resides in Edgewater and directs its young citizens as the elementary school's crossing guard. Her daughter is married to the chief of police.

★   *. . . Richard Seltzer, Esq.?*

After Richard whipped the Donald and collected our commission, he was promoted to senior partner at New York's Kaye Scholer LLP law firm. Richard is still beating bullies as the city's top litigator.

✮ *...418 Undercliff Avenue?*

The Corcoran house was sold in 1978 and is again occupied by three families. The retaining wall is still there, Marty's pool is gone, and the rocks are no longer white.

And here's what's happening with my *Shark Tank* entrepreneurs:

✮ *... **Gayla Bentley**'s designs are now available in more than five hundred stores nationwide and she's in negotiations with QVC.*

✮ *... **Grease Monkey Wipes** doubled their yearly earnings in a single month, and **Erin Whalen** and **Tim Stansbury**'s wipes are now available in every state across the country.*

✮ *... **Pork Barrel BBQ** sauce is sold in more than one thousand grocery and specialty stores nationwide, including Costco, Safeway, and Whole Foods, and **Heath Hall** and **Brett Thompson** have opened their first restaurant.*

✮ *... **Ava the Elephant** is sold in CVS stores across the country. **Tiffany Krumins** fought cancer and won.*

✮ *... **The Body Jac** has been tooled and manufactured, and its infomercial is selling Body Jacs every time it airs. **Cactus Jack** is working on his next invention and still weighs thirty pounds less.*

Credits

Barbara's Heroic Mom

    Florence Corcoran

Barbara's Loving Dad

    Edwin Corcoran

Barbara's Leading Man

    Bill Higgins

Barbara's Business Partner

    Esther Kaplan

Barbara's Literary Agent

    Stuart Krichevsky

Bruce's Costar

    Scott Stewart

Bruce's Guardian Angel

    Raymond Littlefield

Bruce's Cheerleaders

    Winifred and Douglas Bruce

Bruce's Literary Agent

    Todd Shuster

Key Players

    Gail Abrahamsen

    Sylvia Alpert

    Scott Durkin

    Tresa Hall

    Carol Jacobanis

    Lori Levin

    Sheryl Martinelli

    Chelsea Miller

    Anita Perrone

    Bob Sauer

    Rebecca Wood

Secret Counsel

    Ellen Carlson

    T. Corcoran

    Jennifer Henwood

    Lori Higginbotham

    Robert Hoberman

    Ian Lane

    Jennifer Mitchell

    Sy Presten

    Joanne Rooney

Edith Salton

Liz Garland Sauer

Karen Williams

Shark Tank Team

Mark Burnett

Holly Jacobs

Clay Newbill

———

President, Penguin Group (USA)

Susan Petersen Kennedy

Publisher and Editor, Portfolio

Adrian Zackheim

Director of Marketing, Portfolio

Will Weisser

Art Director

Joseph Perez

Assistant Editor

Jillian Gray

Associate Director of Publicity, Portfolio

Allison McLean

Illustrator

John Segal

Interior Designer

Alissa Amell

Special Editor

   Hilary Hinzmann

Audio Director

   Alisa Weberman

Production Editor

   Kate Griggs

And a special thank you to the two thousand incredible people of The Corcoran Group.

Index

Index